CREATING
POSITIVE POLICING NARRATIVES
FOR COUNTERING VIOLENT EXTREMISM

Nadia Gerspacher &
Stevan Weine,
editors

Hedayah
countering violent extremism

ISBN: 978-1-6847-1100-0 (sc)
ISBN: 978-1-6847-1101-7 (e)

Library of Congress Control Number: 2019914921

Lulu Publishing Services rev. date: 10/11/2019

CONTENTS

FOREWORD

It is with the utmost gratitude that I accepted the opportunity to write the foreword for the latest publications in the Community Policing for CVE program, a central pillar of the Hedayah organization since its inception in 2012. Hedayah, the International Center of Excellence for Countering Violent Extremism, was created in response to the growing desire from members of the Global Counterterrorism Forum (GCTF) and the wider international community to establish an independent, multilateral center devoted to capacity-building programs, dialogue, and communications, in addition to research and analysis to counter violent extremism in all its forms and manifestations. We have become a center that can bring together experts, expertise, and experience from around the globe.

Shortly after the foundation of Hedayah, we began a fruitful collaboration with the United States Institute of Peace (USIP), with funding from the U.S. Department of State's Bureau of Counterterrorism and Countering Violent Extremism. This partnership focused on providing a suite of trainings to a multitude of different frontline implementers to support their understanding of their role in countering violent extremism (CVE) and to further their ability to implement programming at the local level. Over the span of three years, the program engaged with civil society actors, educators, media representatives, government officials, and law enforcement personnel from jointly identified priority countries that were directly experiencing the threat of violent extremism. Each bespoke engagement with law enforcement was designed to be both

- *philosophical*—encouraging a change in institutional culture through acceptance that a reliance on overly coercive policing ultimately increases the threat by creating mistrust and antagonizing members of hostile communities; and
- *practical*—providing an opportunity for officers to formulate new approaches for dealing with key aspects of day-to-day policing, such as providing an on-the-ground presence in hostile communities, using stop-and-search tactics, and engaging with minority groups.

The focus on law enforcement was of considerable interest to our organization and to me personally. I was fortunate enough to be raised appreciating and recognizing what a community-oriented policing service looked like, because my mother was the first female police officer in the United Arab Emirates. I witnessed the strength of the relationships she was able to build with those in our community and the resultant trust that was bestowed upon her and colleagues in uniform. While there was the potential that this might result in privileged information being shared with her, it was more important to her that the people she was responsible for serving were confident in her ability to respond in times of need and with the appropriate levels of knowledge and understanding of the issue at hand.

In the CVE context, the transition to more community-based approaches is vital. There is clear evidence that actual or perceived overly coercive policing approaches are a key driver of violent extremism. In areas where the police are seen as discriminatory, corrupt, and/or heavy-handed individuals, young people, especially from marginalized groups, have an increased risk of radicalization and recruitment to violent extremist groups. The community policing model allows for a reliable and mutual flow of information between the public and the police, as well as building effective security partnerships with community leaders and local organizations.

This publication seeks to advance the conversation around community policing by focusing on practical guidance to support international law enforcement agencies as they craft and disseminate narratives around their work. As public scrutiny of law enforcement has increased through the omnipresence of social media, police have had to adapt their communication and outreach to ensure that they are continuing to reach their audience and that concerns around their behavior or response are addressed as quickly as possible. Rather than creating a "counter-narrative" (or a tool that directly or indirectly challenges the ideologies and messages of violent extremism (VE)), this field manual instead explores ways to craft a unique, positive explanation of a police service's vision, mission, and activities as well as ways to ensure that this message is received by the appropriate audiences. This messaging has proven to be effective in combatting the narratives of both supporters of VE and those looking to disrupt the institution of policing by creating and disseminating an honest description of policing activities. Rather than engaging in a verbal sparring match with policing naysayers, this manual instead provides clear guidance on how to capture and publicize strengths within the policing service and how to recognize and admit when some missions may not have gone according to plan.

This manual is a welcome addition to Hedayah's publications, particularly those focused on the importance of strategic communications and the Undermining Violent Extremist Narrative How-to Guides as well as Hedayah's Counter Narrative Library. By focusing on the distinct audience of policing institutions, the content here complements our existing research and programming in a way not previously explored and provides a great deal of potential for future programming with priority countries.

I want to express my sincere thanks to our colleagues at USIP, particularly Dr. Nadia Gerspacher, for initiating and overseeing this process through to publication. A special thanks as well to Mr. Patrick Lynch, director of our Washington, D.C., office, who oversaw the program transition from USIP to our first satellite office. The Community Policing for CVE program would not have been possible without the generous funding contributions from our friends at the U.S. State Department who financed the initial stages of the program and the drafting of this book, as well as at the UK Foreign and Commonwealth Office who continue to support ongoing training initiatives, which are focused on reviewing and revising existing training approaches and curricula. Finally, a huge thanks to all of our partners in law enforcement who have worked alongside us in this program and in the drafting of this material. We thank you both for the courage displayed in your daily work and for your ability to identify ways in which you can continue to improve your service to the community.

Maqsoud Kruse
Executive Director
Executive Office
Hedayah

PREFACE

A critical task in countering violent extremism is to counter the narratives that violent extremist groups (VEGs) use to recruit new followers and radicalize existing ones. The advent of social media and the almost universal access to the Internet has given these messages a worldwide reach. Images and messages of police using, and abusing, their power to employ force have pushed vulnerable individuals toward violent extremist groups. As I experienced firsthand while working with police institutions, the narratives disseminated by violent extremist groups and militants can introduce vocabulary that members of the community, including children and noncombatants such as mothers, adopt when they describe incidents in the community. The language introduced by these groups becomes the language used by those consuming "news" from online sources such as YouTube, Facebook, and Twitter, and it describes police in a very negative light.

Criticism of police operations is not wholly without justification, given the counterterrorism powers police services have been granted and the biases that are alive and well in police institutions, but the critics overlook the fact that police institutions and officers work very hard to protect communities from the threat of attacks by violent extremists. That fact is ignored in no small part because police institutions usually lack the ability to introduce into community discourse what I have come to call a "language of protection." After working with police institutions from Pakistan, Tunisia, Morocco, Jordan, Northern Ireland, and many other places, it became clear to me that the police need to offer communities an alternative vocabulary—one grounded in the principles of protection, safety, service, and collaboration—with which to describe police activities.

The more that communities embrace this language of protection, the more legitimacy they will afford to the police.

Police can either counter or contribute to the radicalization of those vulnerable individuals that violent extremist groups seek to ensnare through their narratives. If they are to counter those messages, police should first recognize that they help shape community narratives through their conduct during operations and patrols and through their general approach toward individuals and groups they encounter in the community for whatever reason. Police institutions typically have internal communications capacities but sometimes lack the capacity to proactively develop a vocabulary with which to describe to the community the work they are doing to protect that community. The police need to shape narratives that not only neutralize violent extremist narratives but also promote a positive impression of the police, emphasizing their protective role and their willingness to partner with, rather than repress, the community, solving their shared problems jointly.

The narratives deployed online and offline by violent extremist groups have been studied widely in recent years. They are now generally understood as storylines diffused through strategic communications to shape existing and potential audiences in order to make those audiences support, tacitly or actively, the extremists' activities. As we conducted research for this book, in the process developing a theory of change to underpin the project, we decided that we would focus on the development of alternative narratives, rather than on counter-narratives. Counter-narratives have been shown to be much less effective than initially hoped, and some experts believe they even contribute to pushing individuals further into violent extremism. The creation of alternative—and, most importantly, positive—narratives is far more promising an approach

This book offers insights and other tools to help police institutions develop narratives that highlight the protection that police provide to their communities. But these tools will be useful only if police institutions are indeed providing such protection and sincerely seek to collaborate with communities for the collective good. The book is not intended to help police institutions present a false description of their activities and intentions. Before being ready to use the insights in this book, police institutions should do the hard work of adopting a community-oriented ethos.

This book embraces the following theory of change: If police understand the nature and scope of influence of violent extremist messages, and also understand why they have influence in a specific context, then the police can formulate alternative messages that leverage what works. Moreover, if police are able to create and implement strategic communication plans around their activities, and these alternative narratives resonate with the communities that the police serve, then radicalization will decrease and communities will see police as partners in building resilience to violent extremists' recruitment.

ACKNOWLEDGMENTS

This project as well as the Policing for CVE program would not have been possible without the support of the U.S. State Department's Bureau of Counterterrorism and Countering Violent Extremism. Its staff are to be applauded for recognizing that professionalizing the police service is an important way for countries to counter the threat of violent extremism. The bureau was a steady and reliable partner throughout the development of the Policing for CVE Program. Special thanks to Oliver Wilcox, Robert McKenzie, Hassan Abbassy, Ayhan Ucok, and Laurie Freeman for their support of the project and for helping to develop the theory of change that is the foundation of the project.

We are grateful to USIP for giving us the space and time to research, develop content and solutions, and write this manuscript. Thank you to Jeff Helsing for including the program and this project in the plans of USIP's Academy for International Conflict Management and Peacebuilding (which enabled this book to be written) and for his constant support.

Thank you to Jessalyn Brogan Walker for her tireless and always enthusiastic contributions, which ranged from administrative support to logistical expertise and editing prowess. Thank you to Nathaniel L. Wilson for his contributions since the beginning of the development of the Policing for CVE Program. Nate surmounted administrative, bureaucratic, political, and organizational hurdles to ensure that police officers from Jordan, Pakistan, Tunisia, Nigeria, Somalia, Kenya, Kosovo, Afghanistan, and many other countries were vetted and were able to travel to attend workshops held in Abu Dhabi, Italy, and Washington, DC.

Special thanks to the authors of this book who travelled to Vicenza,

Italy, to collectively teach a course to test out the validity, usefulness, and applicability of the content of this book. Thank you to Dr. Stevan Weine for helping me put the book together. Thank you to Dr. Stevan Weine, Nathaniel L. Wilson, Jessalyn Brogan Walker, Dr. Dan Waddington, Talene Bilazar, and Stevie Cargin for their hard work in developing this content and bringing their invaluable expertise to this project.

And thank you to the police institutions of Kosovo, Cameroon, Pakistan, Tunisia, Jordan, and Kenya for sending active officers to bring back insights from the course. Their participation and feedback was instrumental in ensuring the maximum relevance of this book's content to current issues that their police services and governments face today.

Nadia Gerspacher
Washington, DC
June 2019

ABOUT THE EDITORS AND CONTRIBUTORS

Editors

Nadia Gerspacher is the former director of security sector education at the Academy for International Conflict Management of the United States Institute of Peace (USIP). Her portfolio included a capacity-building program that enabled her to develop best practices for both implementation and planning. She oversaw projects to identify and disseminate insights, guidelines, knowledge, and skills to security sector audiences in fragile, conflict-affected states. At USIP and elsewhere, she has developed numerous programs to support police reform efforts and security sector reform in general; and has contributed to many partnerships internationally to develop courses, conduct studies, and provide instruction to donor countries and security actors. Her publications include academic studies, technical guides, and applied research and studies to improve foreign assistance and policing practices. She has a PhD in international relations, her research focusing on international police cooperation and on the institutions that facilitate that cooperation. She has also conducted research on the capacity building of police institutions worldwide.

Stevan Weine, MD, is professor of psychiatry at the University of Illinois at Chicago College of Medicine, where he is also director of Global Medicine and director of the Center for Global Health. For twenty-five years, he has been conducting research both with refugees and migrants in the United States and in post-conflict countries, focusing on mental health, health, and violence prevention. He leads an active, externally funded research program that has been supported by multiple federal, state, university, and foundation grants, from 1998 to the present, all with collaboration from community partners. Weine is author of *When History is a Nightmare: Lives and Memories of Ethnic Cleansing in Bosnia-Herzegovina* (Rutgers, 1999) and *Testimony and Catastrophe: Narrating the Traumas of Political Violence* (Northwestern, 2006).

Contributors

Talene Bilazarian is a PhD candidate in political science at the University of Oxford. Her research focuses on the local implementation of and community responses to counter extremism programs in U.S. and UK cities. She has consulted with Hedayah and the United States Institute of Peace to deliver international police training focused on community policing and social media. Her work has appeared in *Lawfare*, George Washington University's Program on Extremism, the Center for Strategic and International Studies, and the journal *Policy & Internet*.

Stephen Cargin is an advisor on strategic leadership, policing, and security who has thirty-three years of policing experience in Northern Ireland and other parts of the world. He is a former assistant chief constable and chief superintendent, Police Service of Northern Ireland Service; a former head and deputy head of the Legacy and Justice Department, Service Improvement Department; and a former district commander, City of Londonderry, one of the most challenging district commands within the United Kingdom. He has significant experience in the service delivery of policing in the context of severe terrorist threats and sectarian conflict and division, including in the role of strategic and tactical commander. He has been closely involved in overt and covert policing operations; police reform; developing and implementing strategies on countering violent extremism; and community engagement involving political leaders and power brokers in volatile, hard-to-reach communities.

Dan Waddington, PhD, has nearly forty years of comprehensive criminal justice experience as a project manager, mentor, consultant, educator, analyst, and practitioner working throughout the United States and in over two dozen other countries. He is a recognized expert in the fields of countering violent extremism, criminal justice reform, community policing, crime analysis, and organization development. He has developed and presented curriculum on many criminal justice topics, and has served as an advisor and guest lecturer for the United States Institute of Peace, the Global Counter Terrorism Forum, and the Hedayah International Centre of Excellence for Countering Violent Extremism. He served as a regional coordinator for the U.S. Department of Homeland Security, developing and expanding efforts at the community level to counter violent extremist recruitment and radicalization to violence. He is currently a professor of criminal justice. He has a bachelor's degree in justice administration, a master's degree in public administration, and a doctorate in Criminal Justice.

Jessalyn Brogan Walker is the program manager of the Community Policing for CVE program at Hedayah and Programs Officer at the Global Center for Cooperative Security. In this position, she works with international police trainers, officers, and leadership to promote community policing as a tool to counter violent extremism. They collaborate to determine opportunities for revising existing in-country police academy curricula to incorporate a community-oriented ethos throughout the training. During her time at the United States Institute of Peace in 2014–2017, she supported the capacity-building program with Hedayah to organize and deliver a host of CVE-relevant workshops and trainings with law enforcement, government, and civil society actors. She holds an undergraduate degree in sociology and politics and a master's degree in criminology from the University College Cork, where she graduated in 2013. Her research interests include international root causes of crime and violence, global prison systems, and identity sensitivity and appreciation.

Nathaniel L. Wilson joined the United States Institute of Peace (USIP) in 2011after stints with the Partnership for Global Security in Washington, DC, and at the Mossawa Center in Haifa, Israel. At USIP, he has coordinated education and training on countering violent extremism (CVE); implemented a project to develop and deliver a CVE curriculum to key civil society and government actors; and coordinated the Policing for CVE program. As the Libya country manager, he leads efforts to support key institutions and build local capacity to undertake peacebuilding and contribute to stabilization and reconciliation in Libya. He has been published in numerous forums and by various institutions, including the Strategic Studies Institute & U.S. Army War College Press and USIP. He holds a master's degree in international relations from American University's School of International Service and a bachelor's degree in political science from the University of Missouri-St. Louis.

CHAPTER 1

INTRODUCTION: SHIFTING THE LANGUAGE ABOUT POLICE

STEPHAN CARGIN, NADIA GERSPACHER, AND JESSALYN WALKER

Communication between a community and its police service is the bedrock of security and safety around the world. The importance of communication is no less when it comes to policing violent extremism and terrorism; indeed, tackling those threats requires a level of professionalism that includes *systematic* communication. However, many police services have retrenched away from regular contact with their communities in the face of the threat of violent extremist and terrorist activity. This retrenchment has resulted in the alienation of communities and police, which in turn has led to both sides vilifying the other and to a dangerous erosion of trust and confidence between them. This rupture in the social contract between the people and the government institution entrusted to protect them provides a haven for violent extremist actors. Violent extremism and terrorism are politically driven activities, and they depend for their community support on a loss of confidence in police and the government. Support for violent extremism can be tacit and may manifest itself through a lack of cooperation and collaboration with the police. But such support can also be active, fueled by the process of radicalization and by a growing and acute sense of whether there is real or perceived grievance among discontented individuals.

Over the last twenty years, violent extremism has become universally recognized as a threat to the safety and security of the international community. As the number of attacks and understanding of the radicalization process leading to violence have grown, increasing attention is being paid to recognizing the structural and individual conditions that lead a person down the path of violent extremism. Although the definition of violent extremism has been contested, in general it refers to the beliefs and actions of people who support or use ideologically motivated violence to further political, religious, or ideological objectives.[1] Those working to counter violent extremism advocate for a comprehensive whole-of-community approach to promote the understanding that all members of a society play a role in identifying and responding to (as appropriate) threats as they arise. A key actor in this space is the police. Police officers have the opportunity to engage with the civilian population in times of stability as well as times of need.

The role of police in countering violent extremism (CVE) cannot be underestimated. Ethical policing models and processes can successfully detect and counter terrorist operations and the behavior of violent extremists. Effective policing has the power to win the hearts and minds of those who are opposed to legitimate law enforcement, creating an environment that embraces police services, thereby enabling better provision of those services. Police officers with access to and an understanding of the larger threat landscape are better equipped both to ensure the safety of an area and to identify potential disruptions. To gain this perspective, however, a police service should first collaborate with the community to foster trust and confidence.

The systematic communication required for a collaborative approach to CVE and terrorism rests in the development of police capacity to create positive narratives, messages that showcase the protection that is provided by police activities. Positive narratives are key to providing a description

---

[1] The United States Agency for International Development (USAID) defines violent extremism as "advocating, engaging in, preparing, or otherwise supporting ideologically motivated or justified violence to further social, economic and political objectives." See USAID, *The Development Response to Violent Extremism and Insurgency* (Washington, DC: USAID, September 2011), 2, https://pdf.usaid.gov/pdf_docs/Pdacs400.pdf.

of police activities and operations that privilege the concept of protection and service. In many communities around the world, police assume that their communities have confidence in their activities. But that is not the case if limited or no communication is directed at communities. CVE depends on sharing information between police and communities for both the prevention of and the response to the use of violence. Police cannot let their actions speak for themselves, because violent extremist groups, militants, and vigilantes are constantly offering the community a negative view of the police, one that focuses on the use of force by police, rather than on the efforts of the police to provide protection.

For example, if police use force during an operation, that use of force may be quickly communicated online and by word of mouth by those seeking to discredit the police and the government. Violent extremists seek to portray police use of force as an abuse of power and a sign that police are not at the service of the community. And this portrayal is likely to resonate within the community in the absence of a police narrative that explains the reason for the use of force and the nature of the operation, using vocabulary of protection rather than of power. Of course, this narrative should be communicated in a context in which there are safeguards for the legitimate use of force; in the absence of such safeguards, any police message is likely to be unpersuasive.

This manual provides police services across the globe with insights on how to create positive narratives that offer a way of understanding their activities as the provision of protection from harm and the creation of safety and security for all. In this manual, we aim to guide police in the development of a language of protection—a language that is different from the police service's current lexicon and that can be adopted by the community to describe the activities of their police service. The language of protection model presented here provides a path to creating positive messages about police activities and an alternative for communities to consider when shaping their opinions about and support for violent extremist groups. The strategy is to shift the language about the police— but that strategy can be effective only if a key condition is first met: police activities and operations should be compliant with the highest level of professionalism possible.

General Principles

To produce this narrative shift, police must collaborate with the community to establish trust and confidence in the police service. Organizational change may be called for in the effort to establish a cycle of public confidence in and two-way engagement between the police and the community and the narratives that reinforce it. To that end, the following six general principles should be borne in mind.

Understand Public Perceptions

It is important that police services understand what the public thinks about the police. To have an accurate, up-to-date understanding of how the police service is perceived, police must gather intelligence, listen to the media, conduct and review opinion surveys, and examine complaint statistics and other performance data. However, these approaches are no substitute to engaging face to face with community members and listening to and understanding what they (particularly those from hard-to-reach communities) think of the police. In fact, assuming one knows how all communities feel about police can be a threat to the very relationships that the organization hopes to build.

Once an understanding of community grievances has been reached, the challenge is determining how the police service is willing and able to respond. Senior police officers must provide the time and space for all staff to understand the perspective of all communities and sub-communities and build opportunities for dialogue, thereby providing both the police and the community with the chance to learn more about and view the humanity of each other.

Work toward a Principled Vision

Each police organization needs to create its own vision and set of governing principles for the delivery of ethical policing and positive narratives around it. Police leaders need to establish clear principles to guide individual and organizational behavior and attitudes. A police organization that defines itself and its members as providers of a service will engage and behave differently than one whose purpose is to identify potential threats to the status quo and to eradicate them.

Having in place a clear set of organizational ethical standards and behaviors is critical for success in changing the community's perception of the police. Ensuring that all staff know what these standards are and that every officer will be personally held accountable for departing from them, is also key. Mechanisms that test compliance and challenge breaches help significantly to demonstrate that the police service is trustworthy and that officers will treat communities with respect.

Create Political Space

For police to make meaningful and lasting progress in building trust and confidence, political leaders must create space to help police succeed. This will be challenging to achieve but it is imperative that the government shows itself willing to make changes to support the larger reform effort. Political leaders, especially those who represent or have influence in hard-to-reach communities, must act as advocates for the police service.

In some countries, the implementation of a national action plan has aided efforts to generate greater support for policing reform efforts. The process of designing and drafting such a plan should promote an inclusive environment in which all relevant stakeholders are consulted, with attention paid to the role of all branches of government as well as police services and civil society organizations. Including language on the role of the police promotes both the political space and the authority to undertake organizational changes that might be necessary as well as illustrating to the larger community that their concerns have been heard and are being addressed. Because the change process can span many years, a document that outlines the process and how it supports larger governance principles can illustrate and provide a benchmark for progress.

Create Narratives

A narrative should not be seen as a static message, but rather as one that is routinely reviewed and revised. Using every opportunity to engage with, listen to, and respond effectively to communities will help ensure that the narrative of the police is in keeping with the needs and expectations of the public. When mistakes are made (as they no doubt will be), the worst thing a police service can do is to try and cover them up. Concealing errors can set trust back many years when the truth eventually comes to light.

Each police service should establish a clear identity for itself and for the community; the service should present itself as having a principled vision and clear sense of direction, with a staff who embody this vision and direction. CVE is a war for public space: violent extremists want to have control of certain areas of the community and to be seen as the only legitimate force within it. The task of the police service is to discredit the violent extremists' claims and to convince the community that it is the only trustworthy and legitimate law enforcement service.

The violent extremist narrative for legitimacy will be in direct competition with the police narrative. Police should not take for granted the high stakes that are at play; they need to be dedicated to peacebuilding and ethical service delivery, an attitude that will save lives—their own and those of community members. Violent extremists want the police to make mistakes, behave inappropriately, and ultimately feed into the extremist narrative, strengthening their own position. Every available opportunity to promote the work and successes of a police service should be seized to further an understanding of and appreciation for the work of the police.

Engender Trust

Trust is not something anyone can expect to enjoy simply because he or she wears a uniform or has a particular rank; it is something that must be earned. Building trust takes time and personal investment, and each officer will be judged by his or her actions. Trust is one of the most powerful narratives an officer can promote. Stories abound about how community leaders and former terrorists have been impacted by the way police officers have treated them. Some have responded to mistreatment by joining or sympathizing with violent extremist groups to exact revenge on the police or on the system they represent. Others have exited those same groups because of positive experiences with police, expressing a desire to work within the bounds of the law to protect and support their communities.

Take Risks

Although the concept of risk is inherent in the field of policing, it is also a critical component of winning support for a police service. By taking risks such as patrolling on foot in hard-to-reach areas, joining a meeting of individuals hostile to the police or the state, or by patrolling so-called no-go areas, a police officer can build positive and enduring relationships with a person or group. Responding to straightforward, local concerns effectively and in a timely manner can significantly enhance such relationships. Actively seeking relationships with people who have influence within a community, particularly those who have influence over sections of the community that have not historically engaged with the police, can be highly rewarding for both individual officers and the larger police service they represent.

How This Manual Is Organized

In July 2017, a workshop on the subject of creating positive policing narratives for CVE was held in Vicenza, Italy, as part of a collaboration between the United States Institute of Peace, the U.S. Department of State, and the Hedayah Centre of Excellence for Countering Violent Extremism. This three-day training was delivered to participants from Kenya, Kosovo, Morocco, Nigeria, Senegal, Tunisia, and Uganda. Throughout the workshop, it became apparent that participants both valued the material being covered and could benefit from a resource that supports the process of crafting and disseminating a narrative.

This manual was compiled with that audience in mind. Chapter 2 introduces the concept of narratives, explains how they are used (by both violent extremist groups and police services), and identifies what makes them effective. Chapter 3 explores how to conduct an organizational assessment that looks at both the strengths and weaknesses of a police service to aid in drafting an effective narrative. Chapter 4 provides guidelines on crafting positive narratives, presenting a step-by-step framework for building community-oriented policing narratives. Chapter 5 discusses how to bring those narratives to the attention of a police service's audiences; the chapter emphasizes the value of directing the messaging to groups beyond the traditional reach of police. Chapter 6 discusses how social media can be used as an effective medium to reach audiences. Chapter 7 highlights the need for an organizational culture that supports and enhances the confidence of the public in the police, thereby reinforcing existing and future narratives. Chapter 8 underlines the key lessons of this manual.

CHAPTER 2

WHY NARRATIVES WORK

NATHANIEL L. WILSON AND STEVAN WEINE

Executive Summary

- Narratives are made of connected stories that provide cognitive and emotional coherence and ultimately impact people's actions.
- To emotionally resonate with audiences, violent extremist narratives claim to provide security, buttress service delivery, and cultivate a sense of culture.
- To resonate in the minds of their audiences, violent extremists use narratives to explain the "in-group" community and the "other," in addition to giving coherence to individual messages.
- Violent extremists motivate action through narratives by providing vision and values, using networks to disseminate narrative, demonstrating credibility of actions, and branding defeat as victory to maintain group morale.
- Police should take proactive steps to create their own narratives that displace those of violent extremists.
- By changing the discourse to offer a compelling vision of the role of police, including with service-oriented actions, police can position themselves as the only legitimate provider of community security.

Introduction

When police leaders reflect on the many activities that make up days, weeks, quarters, and years of successful policing, narratives are likely not at the forefront of their thinking. They may know why a particular officer joined the force, but that knowledge is not critical to understanding actual police work. Stories—war stories—tend to be told after hours, when officers are relaxing and taking time to reflect on enemies bested, escapes narrowly made, obstacles overcome. The best leaders know that personal shared anecdotes are actually an important part of the organization's story. They help officers make sense of the past and push them to take action in the future, informing current and future decision making. Ideally, these stories are a way of learning, and they help mold officers into the best they can be.

Stories give meaning and purpose to actions. Violent extremist organizations realize that narratives are a key component of their strategic toolbox. Two of the most notorious Islamic violent extremist groups, al-Qaeda and DAESH or Daesh, disagreed vehemently on one key narrative aspect: whether or not to broadcast extreme violence as part of their brand. Al-Qaeda feared that examples of brutality such as beheading videos would be used against it by the media. In contrast, Daesh's ideological architect, Abu Musab al-Zarqawi, believed that publishing extreme brutality was necessary to force a schism between Sunni and Shi'a Muslims.[1] A former leader of al-Shabab, al-Qaeda's associates in Somalia, summed up this preoccupation with image, the media, and narrative in 2013: "The war of narratives has become even more important than the war of navies, napalm, and knives."[2]

Facing limited time and financial resources, police leaders may not

---

[1] W. McCants, "The Believer: How an Introvert with a Passion for Religion and Soccer Became Abu Bakr al-Baghdadi, Leader of the Islamic State" (Washington, DC: Brookings Institution, September 1, 2015), http://csweb.brookings.edu/content/research/essays/2015/thebeliever.html. Al-Zarqawi ran al-Qaeda's branch in Iraq from late 2004 until his death in June 2006.

[2] S. Cottee, "Why It's So Hard to Stop DAESH Propaganda," *Atlantic*, March 2, 2015, https://www.theatlantic.com/international/archive/2015/03/why-its-so-hard-to-stop-Daesh-propaganda/386216/.

be convinced of the merits of a focus on narrative development and dissemination. These activities may seem too abstract. Furthermore, even if leadership notionally sees some value to the concept, time dedicated to education and training detracts from time spent honing skills such as training with firearms and practicing arrest procedures. On the job, officers spend so much time dealing with core policing issues of violence and crime that there is little time left for anything else.

Police leaders need to understand that terrorism is more than a crime, and thus approaches to fighting terrorism need to be broader than approaches to fighting crimes such as theft. Violent extremists aim to send a message, to tell a story, and to support a narrative. The number of casualties from violent extremist activities is only one measure of success,[3] and often not the most important. A former officer in charge of the Terrorism Prevention Branch at the United Nations Office on Drugs and Crime, Alex Schmid, elaborates on this idea:

> For too long, terrorism has been understood primarily in terms of (political) violence. Gradually, it has been realized that it should be understood more in terms of communication and propaganda. Violence and propaganda have much in common. Violence aims at behavior modification by coercion. Propaganda aims at the same by persuasion. Terrorism is a combination of the two, using demonstrative public violence as an instrument of psychological warfare, "advertising," as it were, an armed non-state group's capabilities to do harm and to destroy.[4]

Police leadership must look beyond a terrorist crime itself (the message)

---

[3] C. Winter and H. J. Ingram, "Why DAESH Is So Good at Branding Its Failures as Successes," *Atlantic*, September 19, 2017, https://www.theatlantic.com/international/archive/2017/09/Daesh-propaganda/540240/.

[4] Alex P. Schmid, *Al-Qaeda's "Single Narrative" and Attempts to Develop Counter-Narratives: The State of Knowledge* (The Hague: International Center for Counter-Terrorism, 2014), 1, http://www.icct.nl/download/file/AP-Schmid-Al-Qaedas-Single-Narrative-January-2014.pdf.

to understand how violent extremists explain the reasons for the crime (the story) and the larger motivation (the narrative) underlying both. If they do not, then police will be forced to constantly react to bloody events and will not be able to formulate their own narratives to supplant those of violent extremists vis-à-vis the communities they serve. Nothing less than people's minds and hearts are at stake.

Before police can dedicate resources to developing, field testing, refining, and disseminating their own narratives, they must understand the elements of the violent extremist narratives with which they are competing and why these narratives resonate with community members. Police must also understand narratives about police. Without analyzing and truly understanding the narratives that swirl in the community, police will be underequipped to create ones to replace those of the bad actors. Police officers cannot make partnerships or solve community problems without a solid understanding of narratives—violent extremist ones and their own.

This chapter is divided into sections that demonstrate the reasons that narratives impact the minds, hearts, and actions of the intended audience. Each section illustrates how violent extremists recruit and convince recruits to act using narratives. Hearts and minds work together, so the division presented here is not a neat divide. Rather, the classification provides a framework for analyzing violent extremist narratives. The final section touches on an approach that police can take not only to combat violent extremist narratives but also to create alternative ones.

Leaders should not shy away from learning about violent extremist narratives for fear of sympathizing with them. Officers' critical thinking skills, professional training, dedication, and decency are all useful foils to the black-and-white worldview that violent extremists promote.

Narrative Types

Before describing the ways that narratives are effective, it is necessary to define what we mean by "narratives" and their component parts. *Messages* are discreet pieces of information or actions designed to convey information to an audience. *Stories* are made up of more than one message and are "a particular series sequence of related events that are situated in the past and recounted for rhetorical/ideological purposes."[5]

The broadest types of narratives are *master narratives*, which are systems of stories that together provide a coherent view of the world stretching back in time and are deeply embedded in a particular culture.[6] *Narratives* are made up of a coherent system of stories that share a common rhetorical desire to resolve a conflict by establishing audience expectations according to the known trajectories of literary and rhetorical form.[7] A violent extremist narrative can be defined as "a system of stories that hang together to provide a coherent view of the world for the purpose of supporting individuals, groups, or movements to further illegal violent and violence-assisting activities."[8]

One common way of looking at narratives is to distinguish among dominant narratives, counternarratives, and alternative narratives. *Dominant narratives* are the stories told by the dominant culture; they define reality and guide lives like an invisible hand. *Counter-narratives* are arguments that dispute a commonly held belief or truth. *Alternative narratives* are stories that hang together to provide a coherent view of the world that displaces, without directly confronting, the dominant narrative. Police need to create alternative narratives that build new sources of legitimacy and are associated with community-oriented approaches toward countering violent extremism, including community policing.[9]

Successful organizations—both violent extremist and police ones—understand the interrelated nature of these tools as important for recruiting people from certain cultures with specific histories. The key point is that all narratives are made up of stories that are repeated through networks,

---

[5] Jeffry R. Halverson, H. L. Goodall, Jr., and Steven R. Corman, *Master Narratives of Islamist Extremism* (New York: Palgrave Macmillan, 2011), 13.

[6] Ibid., 14.

[7] Stevan Weine, "Narrative Principles for Community Policing Regarding Violent Extremism" (presentation at the conference Creating Positive Policing Narratives for CVE: A Leadership Course for Police Institutions, Vicenza, Italy, July 18, 2017.

[8] A. Beutel et al., "Guiding Principles for Countering and Displacing Extremist Narratives," *Journal of Terrorism Research* 7, no. 3 (2016): 35–49, http://doi.org/10.15664/jtr.1220.

[9] Weine, "Narrative Principles."

and when organizations effectively tell their stories, they have the power to gain people's support.

Emotional Appeal

People are not computers: they are not data-processing machines driven purely by cold logic. Humans are motivated by emotional factors as well. The fact that recruits to violent extremist organizations do not act rationally should not be used as an excuse to give into the temptation to conclude that they are crazy.

People make choices based on rational understanding as well as emotions. So why do narratives touch the hearts of their audiences? They do so by meeting the human needs for security, essential services, and culture.

Desire for Security

Powerful emotional symbols can make meaningful contributions to efforts to win people's loyalty. For example, extremist groups want to position themselves as the group in society that represents and offers justice or security. If they can make a claim that the government is not the legitimate provider of justice or security, then their emotional pull is strengthened.

Depending on the context, economic conditions may be a motivating factor for joining a violent extremist group. The pitch is not necessarily, "You're poor, you'll get a job if you join." But improving people's lives, even if temporarily, by giving them money and a job does enhance the emotional appeal by meeting people's needs. For example, a UN study found that the majority of people who joined an extremist group were frustrated economically and a job was their biggest need. The prospect of a job, combined with feelings of "hope/excitement" as well as "anger," "vengeance," and "fear," can be a potent enticement.[10]

An example of an explicit emotional appeal is DAESH's slogan *Baqiyya*

---

[10] United Nations Development Programme, *Journey to Extremism in Africa: Drivers, Incentives, and the Tipping Point for Recruitment* (New York: United Nations, 2017), http://journey-to-extremism.undp.org/.

wa tatamaddad (Arabic for "staying and expanding"). It implies that Daesh is in the process of building something. It is not satisfied with the status quo, and it is doing what it can to change it. The grand ambition is to abolish the nation-state system and establish a global caliphate, the Islamic notion of an empire led by a pious leader. Note that Daesh is not simply countering the status quo—it is presenting an alternative to it. This narrative appeals especially to younger people, who tend to want to live out ambitious, large ideas. Moreover, it is inherently positive in the sense that it gives people the idea that they are part of something larger than themselves, something with a purpose. This adds up to a sense of individuals having purpose, agency, and meaning in their life.[11] Combined with a sense of adventure, this is a powerful draw, and it should not be underestimated.

Even when Daesh was being pushed back militarily and losing territory, it was putting forth the narrative, through song, that, "our State has made the tears of our enemies flow. Our gale wind has dispersed them, killed them by the thousands, and led them to their deaths."[12]

Need for Essential Services

Police know that gangs and drug cartels use service provision as a strategy to build the support of local communities. This is true even if people do not appreciate some of the services being provided, like the Mafia in Sicily providing "protection" to local businesses at a price. But other services are welcome, particularly in places where security or justice is lacking or police are perceived poorly. By looking at the needs of communities and seeking to fulfill them, violent extremists engage in simple and effective problem solving with communities.

---

[11] Scott Atran, "The Role of Youth in Countering Violent Extremism and Promoting Peace" (address to UN Security Council, Ministerial Debate, April 23, 2015, https://www.unisa.edu.au/Global/EASS/MnM/Publications/Address_UN_Security_Council_Scott_Atran.pdf.

[12] A. Meuse, "As DAESH Gets Squeezed in Syria and Iraq, It's Using Music as a Weapon," National Public Radio, June 29, 2017, https://www.npr.org/sections/parallels/2017/06/29/533803886/as-Daesh-gets-squeezed-in-syria-and-iraq-its-using-music-as-a-weapon.

For example, there have been reports that al-Shabab in Somalia has gathered support by functioning as a shadow government in the areas it controls. It places itself as the legitimate provider of justice and security by offering safety in its territories, mobile courts for resolving disputes, and enforcement of laws. Its structure is decentralized and local, so its narrative as defender of marginalized and disenfranchised groups can be highly contextualized. It has worked with clans to encourage and manipulate grievances, partner with antigovernment militias, and generally embed itself within society in a way that has made it look and act in ways indistinguishable from a civilian administration. It has also run a system of taxation.[13]

Although it is clear to outside observers that al-Shabab is not the legitimate authority in Somalia, to locals it might not be so clear. Indeed, al-Shabab has become "the main alternative to the government." When there is a choice between corrupt officials and armed groups that are not as exploitive, locals may logically choose the armed groups. And if these groups garner goodwill by providing services, then attitudes toward the groups are more likely to be positive. Taking al-Shabab as an example, there are reports that it controls roads and collects tolls without some of the bribery and corruption typical of police in some parts of the world. Al-Shabab reportedly even offers receipts.[14]

When violent extremist groups offer communities something that they are missing, and thereby gain support, their narratives are reinforced. Locals may make the calculation that it is a rational choice to support the group, and the goods and services it offers create emotional attachments. When the government, the police, or the international community then confronts the group, locals are more likely to either actively or passively support the group.

---

[13] Tricia Bacon, "This Is Why Al-Shabaab Won't Be Going Away Anytime Soon," *Washington Post*, July 7, 2017, https://www.washingtonpost.com/news/monkey-cage/wp/2017/07/06/this-is-why-al-shabaab-wont-be-going-away-any-time-soon/?utm_term=.94effe76a767.

[14] Ibid.

Cultural Cravings

Police leaders know that the culture of their organization is fundamental to how their officers interact with members of the community. The ways that officers interact with each other off duty and the ways they go about doing their job contribute to the culture of the organization. Culture goes beyond police policies, procedures, and compensation. It extends to the way officers greet each other, what they eat, how they talk about their jobs, the music they listen to, and what they discuss when they are not talking about work—in other words, everything that is not directly, specifically related to carrying out the primary duties of the job has an impact on organizational culture.

Violent extremist organizations have much the same situation. An extremist's day is not made up entirely of drilling, studying, and other task-oriented militant activity. Members of violent extremist groups such as DAESH have lives outside of their organizational roles. But the two are connected. As scholar Thomas Hegghammer, who has studied Daesh 's culture, relays:

> It's basically a very sensitive aesthetic [cultural] universe we're dealing with, with poetry, singing, art, graphic art, visual art and a whole lot of religious rituals—a lot of things that seem to have no purpose, no kind of military function. And this is what got me interested in this to begin with. It was that you had these hunted men— because terrorists are hunted men. They're short on time and resources. And you should expect them to spend all their time on useful things like building bombs or writing propaganda or raising funds. But here they are doing all these seemingly useless things. And that I thought was really, really fascinating.

The "useless things" that Hegghammer studies strengthen the bonds that fighters have with each other in ways that animate group dynamics and strengthen ideas in ways that rational thought alone cannot express. He explains:

There's been a tendency to think about radicalization as the result of . . . [a] cognitive process, that they are persuaded by the force of argument of a given doctrine. Whereas . . . there's also a sort of aesthetic seduction going on, that there is a process here that doesn't necessarily involve the mind or the cognition as much as the heart and emotions. And that . . . is an important insight.

Violent extremist groups place a high priority on cultural elements. "Ironically, the violent extremists already understand the value of culture," Ambassador (ret.) Cynthia Schneider explains. "And that's why they attack it. . . . They recognize it as the root of identity and community."[15] She tells a story of how locals in Timbuktu went to great lengths to hide and move ancient, religiously inspired transcripts when al-Qaeda invaded in 2012. Al-Qaeda imposed a strict version of Islamic law, one that ran counter to the local culture and tradition embodied in the transcripts. These transcripts were "a treasure trove of knowledge. They contain treatises on human rights, women's rights, philosophy, scientific exploration, religion, poetry and music. Together, they make up a powerful, authentic, religious-based counter-narrative to extremism."[16] They were thus dangerous to the narrative propagated and imposed on the locals by al-Qaeda. Hence, al-Qaeda wanted to destroy the transcripts to erase memories of history and other interpretations of religion and wipe the slate clean for the imposition of new rules and identities.

When the original identity has been demolished, it can be replaced by whatever the extremists hope to insert. This requires a narrative that skews or erases the past and explains the present from the violent extremists' perspective.

Violent extremists make stories resonate not by a monotonous recounting of facts, but through artistic ways that touch emotions. Storytelling is an art form as old as humankind. From primitive cultures' telling of tales of the glorious victories of the tribe to modern Hollywood

---

[15] Cynthia Schneider, "Extremists Get Why Culture Matters. Why Don't We?" (TEDx talk, TEDxMidAtlantic, October 30, 2015), https://www.youtube.com/watch?v=l2RbImeUVqw.
[16] Ibid.

and *Star Wars*, humans understand what is good and what is not good by telling and listening to stories. When moral judgments are asserted, people can act in ways that support their understanding of right and wrong based on the stories they know and the narratives they subscribe to.

Appeal to Minds

Narratives are effective at influencing people's thoughts—their minds—because they tell people what groups they belong to and what groups are the "other" (and are enemies), and they offer a way to make sense of facts and justify why people support some organizations and oppose others.

Affirm the In-Group

Violent extremist narratives give recruits the message loud and clear that they are members of the community. The "community" for extremist groups is often a broad cross-section of the population, whether it is Islamic violent extremist groups, white people (for white supremacists), workers (for communists), and so on. Extremists often frame their narratives in grand terms using master narratives.

An inclusive message can make even honest, law-abiding citizens pause when considering which groups to support. The narrative of inclusiveness and highlighting of grievances can make individuals consider arguments that they might otherwise have rejected. The group of people "on the fence" is the very group that both police and violent extremists fight for.[17] Which side of the fence wins the fence-sitters' loyalty may hinge on dominant narratives that help citizens understand their places in society and allow them to feel included or marginalized.

But although violent extremists use narratives to target a wide group initially, they also narrow messages to focus on those who might carry out violence. Violent extremist groups are the exception—the extreme—to the wider group of people who engage in political protest. Communities

---

[17] People who are sympathetic or acquiescent to the ideas, aims, and actions of violent extremists.

often have a large amount of people who have grievances and are willing to use legitimate, nonviolent means of expressing their protest. The violent members of the group will use force in order to separate themselves from their nonviolent counterparts and force people who are protesting to choose sides. When there is such separation, the violent group is left with the most committed supporters. If members of this group try to understand the perspective of the government—the police, politicians, and the like— comrades see it as a betrayal.[18] There is an active reinforcement of the narrative of defending the group and a deepening of the radicalization of its members.

To reinforce organizational and community culture, the most effective groups find ways, large and small, to show appreciation for the efforts of their members. For example, Daesh had a huge cadre of social media supporters before tech companies began purging platforms of content. Daesh did not take these supporters for granted and dubbed the active broadcasters of propaganda "knights of the upload."[19]

While this title might sound silly, for those who put in time and energy to support Daesh's cause, such labeling could have the effect of radicalizing them further. The thrill of recognition from institutions or leaders is something effective police leaders understand well. Not only do encouragement and public praise tell people what behavior is rewarded, but also they tighten the bonds of brotherhood in the organization.

Moreover, for people unused to receiving praise of this kind, recognition and the familial ties that hardcore violent extremist groups provide might pull them toward the group. This is true especially for people who do not find affirmation in other experiences. Affirmation and the promise of being part of a community are powerful draws for marginalized and disaffected people. But they are also powerful forces for large groups of well-adjusted people who crave community.

---

[18] M. Sageman, *How People Become Terrorists*, March 1, 2017 (Washington, DC: New America), https://www.newamerica.org/international-security/events/how-people-become-terrorists/.

[19] Cottee, "Why It's So Hard."

Name the "Other"

The most inclusive narratives have a corresponding exclusionary side. They place Muslims against the West, Jews versus Palestinians, Sunni battling Shi'a, or white opposing black. A "with-us-or-against-us," "us-versus-them" narrative creates a mentality where members of the organization see themselves as standing athwart an enemy. As Alejandro Beutel, a researcher who has studied extremists, explains, extremists "often tend to think in very black-and-white ways rather than in much more complex, gray ways."[20] This idea extends to entire groups of people who are part of the "other." Narratives create or reinforce this mentality.

Arno Michaels of Life after Hate, a group that helps individuals exit from violent extremist groups, says of his thinking during his time in the white supremacist movement, "It was revealed to me that white people are my people."[21] This is an interesting choice of words: he uses the passive voice as if he had no choice in the matter of which group was his in-group. This is how violent extremist groups want people to receive their messages, as if they are being handed down unquestioned and unquestionable truth. "We literally had blinders up [in order] to deny all this information from the world around us that indicated other people were as human as we were."[22] This mental rigidity is strengthened through narratives and the social dynamics of the groups themselves, including their cultural practices.

The Concept of Legitimacy

Violent extremist groups localize their messages so people question the legitimacy of police. If the community loses faith in the police and the government as the legitimate provider of security, then a void is created that violent extremists and others can try to fill. The concept of legitimacy

---

[20] Anna Almendrala, "This Is How White Supremacists Get Radicalized," *Huffington Post*, August 14, 2017, http://www.huffingtonpost.com/entry/white-supremacists-radicalized-experts_us_59922ba2e4b090964299595b?ncid=inblnkushpmg00000009.

[21] NoPawn, *Whatever Happened to Arno of White Power Band Centurion? YouTube*, May 7, 2011, https://www.youtube.com/watch?v=0EembbNP3j0.

[22] Ibid.

is crucial to understand because it refers to the psychological state of mind of members of the community:

> [Legitimacy is] the belief that authorities, institutions, and social arrangements are appropriate, proper, and just. This quality is important because when it exists in the thinking of people within groups, organizations, or societies, it leads them to feel personally obligated to defer to those authorities, institutions, and social arrangements.[23]

Violent extremist organizations want to dispute the fact that police and security services are the rightful providers of security. Therefore, a key tactic is to use narratives to drive a wedge between communities and police. Narratives that portray police as corrupt, self-interested, only protecting the status quo, or militarized can all be effective in eroding the trust that communities feel toward police—enhancing doubt that police are working for the betterment of the community.

In response to terrorist threats, police might feel they need to take harsh actions such as imposing curfews or rounding up suspects. Indeed, the purpose of violent extremists, and the narratives they employ, is, according to David Lake, to "provoke the target [in this example, the police or the government] into a disproportionate response, radicalize moderates and build support for its objectives in the long term."[24] Researchers interviewed more than five hundred former violent extremists in Africa for a UN study and found that "government action" such as the "killing of a family member or friend" or the "arrest of a family member or friend" was the turning point for joining a violent group.[25] When combined with other factors, such as ideological radicalization and economic marginalization,

---

[23] Tom Tyler, "Psychological Perspectives on Legitimacy and Legitimation," *Annual Review of Psychology* 57, no. 1 (2006): 375.

[24] David Lake, "Rational Extremism: Understanding Terrorism in the Twenty-first Century," *Dialog-IO* 1, no. 1 (spring 2002).

[25] J. Burke, "African Governments' Actions Push People into Extremism, Study Finds," *Guardian*, September 7, 2017, https://www.theguardian.com/world/2017/sep/07/african-governments-actions-push-people-into-extremism-study-finds?CMP=Share_iOSApp_Other.

perceived abuses by a state's security forces clearly push people to join groups.

Terrorist attacks bring legitimacy issues to the forefront. The implicit message terrorists send is that police and government cannot protect the community or country. If violent extremists have laid the groundwork to diminish public confidence and trust in police, then community members will be less likely to see police as being on their side and may even think that police will make things worse when they are called. Members of the community are then predisposed to regard an incident with police involving force, even one completely justified, in the worst light possible.

Connect the Dots

Even the best narratives have holes and compete with other narratives to explain events. People process a great deal of data and a large number of messages every day, but without a way to put these details together to explain the meanings behind these messages, they are just disconnected pieces of information. Much like a detective takes pieces of evidence to tell the tale of how and why someone committed a crime, people use narrative to add context to information so it fits into a coherent story with a plausible explanation. In this way, extremist groups do the detective work for their followers by connecting different pieces of the narrative and dictating to people how they should interpret events.

When told effectively, narratives allow people to take any fact and put it in the story they have been told. Violent extremist leaders do not want their followers looking for the unvarnished truth. They do not want them connecting facts themselves to construct their own stories. Instead, violent extremists want people to know the extremist version of what the past has been and where the future is heading, and then situate the present within these periods. Of course, the present must be in line with what the violent extremists hope to accomplish.

For followers to accept leaders' versions of events, narratives must ring true to their audiences. Take al-Qaeda, for example, whose narratives "possess an internal coherence" for supporters and recruits "that connects them to grand, deeply culturally embedded, views of history—to master narratives—that Muslim audiences, in broad terms, readily understand, identify with, or feel little need to question."[26] The stage is set for specific messages or stories to bring recruits into the fold and reinforce the loyalty that individual members feel toward the organization.

Motivate Action

The previous sections discuss why narratives are able to grab hold of people's thoughts, ideas, and imaginations. In many jurisdictions, people have the freedom to believe what they want to believe and even to express extremist ideas. The police cannot monitor the private thoughts of individuals, nor should the police try to do so.

However, the international community has decided that individuals and groups cannot, for any reason, use violence to carry out ideological or political aims. The twenty-nine member countries and the European Union that make up the Global Counterterrorism Forum (GCTG) agree that terrorist violence is unacceptable. The United Nations has rejected terrorism in all its forms. So although it is crucial for police to understand extremist narratives and why they resonate, before police design their own, alternative narratives they must realize that policing thought is not the end game. Rather, the goals are to persuade people to comply with the law and to dismantle the rationale for and emotional appeal of terrorism.

What distinguishes a terrorist act from a run-of-the-mill crime such as burglary is the motivation behind the crime. Terrorists use violence to achieve their objectives and change the status quo. Violence is intended to breed more violence by convincing others of its effectiveness and by provoking the use of force by the police, further alienating community members.

Thus, because violent extremist narratives help spread violence, police need to have effective strategies to stop, roll back, or replace these narratives. How do terrorists spread violence through narratives? They do so by justifying members' actions, building networks to disseminate narratives, demonstrating group credibility, and using a formidable ability to spin victory from obvious defeat.

---

[26] Halverson, Goodall, and Corman, *Master Narratives*, 13.

Justify Action through Vision and Values

Extremist narratives offer people an opportunity think of their actions as part of something larger than themselves.[27] Narratives explain people's inclusion in community, and they also provide the rationale for individuals' actions and the actions of the group as a whole.

We have all been part of organizations that seem rudderless, where the leadership is not clear about what the mission is or why it matters. Without a narrative acting as the adhesive to bind together activities and vision, an organization will drift and individuals will be left with vague, unactionable ideas. Without a vision and narratives, individuals are left guessing as to what their actions mean on a day-to-day basis.

President John F. Kennedy famously proposed that the United States "should commit itself to achieving the goal, before the decade is out, of landing a man on the moon and returning him safely to the earth."[28] Legend has it that President Kennedy was visiting the headquarters of the National Air and Space Agency when he saw a janitor mopping the floor and walked over to ask what he was doing. The janitor replied, "Well, sir, I'm helping to put a man on the moon!" With President Kennedy's clear goal, everyone at the agency knew the vision, and no matter what their specific task was at any point, they were all pulling in the same direction. There is no doubt that a clear goal and vision can elevate the most mundane work to loftier status.

Vision becomes even more powerful when it is combined with higher values. Researchers have found that that many fighters for Daesh and for the Kurdistan Worker's Party were motivated to join and fight by values

---

[27] Scott Atran, Hammad Sheikh, and Angel Gomez, "Devoted Actors Sacrifice for Close Comrades and Sacred Cause," *Proceedings of the National of Sciences of the United States of America*, December 3, 2014, http://www.pnas.org/content/111/50/17702.full.

[28] John F. Kennedy Presidential Library and Museum, *JFK in History: Space Program*, https://www.jfklibrary.org/learn/about-jfk/jfk-in-history/space-program.

that they deemed non-negotiable (so-called sacred values). These fighters were even willing to forsake their families for these values.[29]

The need to justify actions is a part of both rational thought and emotional motivation. The idea of being part of something larger than oneself is powerful, and fighting for a cause can be downright irrational. As social beings, humans convey motivations, desires, and ideas through social networks, which can have powerful effects on people's actions.

Build and Use Networks

The world's understanding of how information is disseminated and impacts social change has shifted over time. The understanding of information as being injected into the minds of passive recipients (the "hypodermic needle" model), together with the notion that opinion leaders play a powerful role (the "two-step flow" model), has been replaced with a new paradigm characterized by connectivity, a proliferation of media channels and sources of information, and active audiences.

> The Internet's centrality as a means of communication now means that messages crafted for one particular audience often end up being viewed by many other audiences as well, which adds an additional layer of complexity to the development of strategic communication campaigns. In other words, in an increasingly interconnected world, a series of messages intended for a specific audience can have a positive impact on that audience but inadvertently have a negative impact on another, unintended audience.[30]

To avoid a negative impact, Daesh and other extremist organizations

---

[29] Ángel Gómez, Lucía López-Rodríguez, Hammad Sheikh, Jeremy Ginges, Lydia Wilson, Hoshang Waziri, Alexandra Vázquez, Richard Davis, and Scott Atran, "The Devoted Actor's Will to Fight and the Spiritual Dimension of Human Conflict," *Nature Human Behavior* 1 (2017): 6.

[30] N. C. Fink and J. Barclay, *Mastering the Narrative: Counterterrorism Strategic Communication and the United Nations* (New York: Center on Global Counterterrorism Cooperation, 2013), 16.

employ messaging that varies from place to place. It is tuned effectively according to the drivers or factors that motivate people in each community. People become victims of extremist recruitment processes because extremists' messages resonate with their particular culture and grievances.

It is important to understand the nexus between narratives and the networks of people that create, sustain, and disseminate. Narratives are inseparable from networks. As Cristina Archetti elucidates:

> [A] narrative does not exist in a void. If it exists, it is because the story it embodies is told and continuously re-told by the people who belong to that network. Understanding this is important: sending a "narrative" into the information environment (as [some] current approaches in fact aim to do) without there being a network to convey it and re-convey it could be compared to sending a message into outer space. What should then be remembered is that narratives are not made [just] by words, but by social practices.[31]

These social practices and face-to-face interactions are important to underscore. There is evidence that many people are recruited by people they know well. For instance, recruits to the Red Brigade terrorist group in the 1970s were often influenced by peers or family members.[32] Another example is from a 2009 study of European recruits to al-Qaeda in the 1990s and 2000s that showed that 75 percent of recruitment was done by friends and another 20 percent by family members; strangers accounted for

---

[31] C. Archetti, "Terrorism, Communication, and New Media: Explaining Radicalization in the Digital Age," *Perspectives on Terrorism* 9, no. 1 (February 2015): 49–59.

[32] Donatella Della Porta, "Leftwing Terrorism in Italy," in *Terrorism in Context,* ed. Martha Crenshaw (University Park: Pennsylvania State University Press, 1995), 105–59; and Kim Cragin, Melissa A. Bradley, Eric Robinson, and Paul S. Steinberg, *What Factors Cause Youth to Reject Violent Extremism? Results of an Exploratory Analysis in the West Bank* (Santa Monica, CA: RAND Corp., 2015), 3, https://www.rand.org/pubs/research_reports/RR1118.readonline.html.

only 5 percent of successful recruitment activities.[33] Indeed, as Mohammed Hafiz explains, "Individuals that join violent groups often do so because they have one or more family members or friends in the movement. Radicalization and recruitment are local and highly personal tasks involving interpersonal ties, bonds of solidarity, and trust."[34] Similarly, a study of Palestinians found that families were the most persuasive actors when it came to convincing potential recruits of the merits of *staying away from* v*iolence.*[35] These studies suggest that successful efforts at recruitment use narratives to build on shared connections.

But recruitment methods vary over time based on the situational needs of the organization. Networks can be formal, as in police organizations, or more informal. Nafees Hamid explains a couple of different recruitment models:

> As the structures of terrorist organizations evolve so too do their recruitment methods. In failed states, such as Syria, groups take on a hierarchical "command-cadre" structure, which resembles a formal military and allows the group to operate openly while providing security and governance in the area it controls. For some inhabitants of such areas, joining them may be more a matter of practicality than of conviction. In developed nations, such as in Europe, terrorist groups must operate clandestinely and thus take on a "network" structure. Networks are self-organizing, though they often contain charismatic

---

[33] N. Hamid, "What Makes a Terrorist?," *New York Review of Books*, August 23, 2017, https://www.nybooks.com/daily/2017/08/23/what-makes-a-terrorist/.

[34] Mohammed Hafez and Creighton Mullins, "The Radicalization Puzzle: A Theoretical Synthesis of Empirical Approaches to Homegrown Extremism," *Studies in Conflict & Terrorism* 38, no. 11 (2015): 964.

[35] K. Cragin, M. A. Bradley, E. Robinson, and P. S. Steinberg, *What Factors Cause Youth to Reject Violent Extremism? Results of an Exploratory Analysis in the West Bank* (Santa Monica, CA: RAND Corp., 2015), https://www.rand.org/pubs/research_reports/RR1118.html.

leaders who pull together disparate individuals and small groups of friends.[36]

This final point is important to make because the charismatic leaders Hamid mentions are able to send messages in ways that touch both the hearts and the minds of audience members. Charisma can be natural, cultivated by means such as body language and tone. It can also be earned through experience; the veneer of expertise, for example, can be a powerful attractor. But even the most powerful orator, able to make passionate arguments that appeal to logic and emotion, is undermined by hypocrisy. Leadership comes through demonstrated credibility of matching words with actions.

Demonstrate Credibility

As should be clear by now, narratives are effective only when they go beyond words. The stories must match what people observe in their own experiences. If there is a disjointedness, then groups open themselves to charges of hypocrisy. Only the most extreme supporters of a group are able to overlook actions of groups that do not correspond to what the group preaches. Because both violent extremist groups and police want the support of people who are driven by logic and emotion, there is a need to align words and actions.

Sometimes the more audacious the action, the more impact it can have. DAESH seeks to do away with nation-states and instead establish a global caliphate. This notion has a strong appeal for many Muslims, so, although DAESH may not be what they imagine when they think of as restoring a caliphate, the goal is a noble one in many minds (yet little understood by non-Muslims).[37] DAESH disseminated a video of its militants bulldozing

---

[36] S. Hamid, "The Roots of the Islamic State's Appeal," *Atlantic,* October 31, 2014, https://www.theatlantic.com/international/archive/2014/10/the-roots-of-the-islamic-states-appeal/382175/?single_page=true.

[37] Ibid.

the Sykes-Picot line, the modern border between Iraq and Syria[38]. This powerful symbolic message told people that DAESH is serious about achieving its goals. Unlike some groups that talk big but take no action or are hypocritical, DAESH took action to back up its words and used the evidence to reinforce its narrative of restoring the caliphate. That narrative is unlikely to evaporate quickly. Even now, as DAESH is pushed out of Iraq and Syria, it is calling for recruits in Southeast Asia to join its fighters in Indonesia.[39]

Despite its failure to establish a global caliphate, DAESH scored a huge propaganda victory via its recruitment drive. One credible source estimates that 31,000 people from eighty-six countries had traveled to Iraq and Syria as of September 2016 to support DAESH or another extremist group. This number boosts DAESH's claims of having global appeal, of being able to disseminate a message to the worldwide community of Muslims, despite a subsequent drop off in recruitment and battlefield defeat.

Spin Defeat as Victory

The idea that everything will work out in the end is an extremely powerful message. It can boost morale at the worst of times and reinforce good outcomes. Belief in a positive destiny can neutralize emotions and spur action both at peaks and valleys.

American settlers knew this when they pushed westward in the nineteenth century and encountered Indians who fought back against encroachment on their lands. The Indians used violence by scalping their victims and brutally attacking the invaders. But the Americans believed that their fate was to conquer vast stretches of the North American

---

[38] The Sykes-Picot line, agreed in secret by the British and the French in 1916 "the Syria-Iraq border"; a "colonial convention" to build the so-called "New Middle East", an entity to replace what was known as the Arab nation, based on the fragmentation of the region's countries along sectarian, ethnic and religious lines".
[39] "DAESH Recruits Fighters for the Philippines Instead of Syria," *NBC News*, September 12, 2017, https://www.nbcnews.com/storyline/Daesh-uncovered/Daesh-recruits-fighters-philippines-instead-syria-n796741?utm_content=bufferc2ee8&utm_medium=social&utm_source=twitter.com&utm_campaign=buffer.

continent, a purpose referred to as "Manifest Destiny." So even while they were defeated in specific instances, the settlers continued to believe that the continent was rightfully theirs. This widely held vision allowed for people in search of land to brave the frontier. Moreover, even those who thought that their fellow Americans were treating the Native American harshly—attacking them on and cheating them out of their own land— were unwilling to concede the idea that the continent would inevitably be part of the United States. The powerful idea took hold, and people followed this narrative on trails and railroads as they conquered what became the western United States.[40]

Islamic violent extremists have a potent tool in their toolbox that is hard for non-Muslims to understand and problematic to replicate. This is the idea that no matter what happens—tragedy, victory, defeat—it is God's will. Defeat can be explained as temporary and victory is seen as a sign that the extremists are operating in God's path. Whatever is happening, it was meant to happen, and all one can do is to strive to fulfill God's will. While the idea of divine fate is common to all Muslims (a common Arabic phrase, *inshallah*, means "if God wills it"), DAESH has hijacked this belief to justify atrocities against decency and fellow Muslims.

As these two examples demonstrate, a strongly held belief in a narrative affects people's actions. Americans settled the West in the face of reports of terrifying opposition because of a belief in their destiny (although personal ambition and other motivating factors no doubt were influential). DAESH uses a belief in fate to keep fighters motivated and to steady its narrative in the face of external events, even ones that appear catastrophic to the uninitiated.

It is easy to understand why people who have unshakeable beliefs in the righteousness of their cause—true believers—do not easily renounce them, even when facts contradict those beliefs. The deep investment that people make in their groups—devoting time, resources, and brainpower— means that renouncing beliefs comes at a high cost. Many people are not willing to pay this fee, especially if it means that their reputation will be dented. In the case of DAESH recruits, particularly international fighters

---

[40] S. C. Gwynn, *Empire of the Summer Moon: Quanah Parker and the Rise and Fall of the Comanches, the Most Powerful Indian Tribe in American History* (New York: Scribner, 2011).

who joined battles in Iraq and Syria, they have cut ties with family and friends and sold all their possessions and burning their passports. These true believers have created new social groups to reinforce their beliefs.[41] Conscious that the recruits are unlikely to abandon their newfound "truths," the security services of their countries of origin do not welcome them home; for example, the British have stripped fighters of citizenship.[42] All these factors, including the fact that recruits have used or supported violence, mean that logistically and mentally it is difficult for those who have joined an extremist group to quit it.

Proactive Police Narratives

Thus far, the discussion has focused on the narratives told by violent extremists, which are central to inspiring and perpetuating terrorism. Generally, any narrative can be effective if it touches the hearts and minds of people and contains the possibility of causing action. But why do violent extremists' narratives work on people's emotions? The reasons include answering human longing for security and related services, as well as satisfying the desire for shared cultural practices. Why do they work on people's minds? Narratives tell individuals which groups they belong to and which they do not, in addition to giving a mental framework for understanding events in everyday life. Violent extremists spread violence by promulgating distorted values and visions of the world, using extensive networks with credible actions and leaders and twisting ideology to explain everything as part of a master plan.

Now we are going to pivot to briefly consider the narratives told by police officers, which can be central to the work of preventing terrorism. Police use narratives to establish the legitimacy of their efforts with the public, in the process having to address serious questions and concerns

---

[41] J. Keating, "DAESH's End-of-the-World Problem," *Slate,* September 13, 2017, http://www.slate.com/articles/technology/future_tense/2017/09/Daesh_s_ apocalyptic_prophecies_aren_t_coming_true.html.

[42] "UK 'Has Stripped 150 Jihadists and Criminals of Citizenship,'" *Guardian,* July 30, 2017, https://www.theguardian.com/uk-news/2017/jul/30/uk-has-stripped-150-jihadists-and-criminals-of-citizenship.

about police intentions and practices. In particular, the use of community-oriented policing is supported by a strategically crafted narrative that casts the police as protectors of communities from all forms of violence, including political violence, and as civil servants who can build community resilience. To support this narrative, police must have an understanding of the roles of storytelling and the principles of narratives as they relate to community-oriented policing, which subsequent chapters explore in detail. Here, however, we can briefly mention two narrative principles that can help police begin to think about how to replace violent extremist narratives. One principle is to change the conversation—to shift the subject or focus of a narrative from a subject that, for example, calls into question a police service's legitimacy in the eyes of the community to a topic that spotlights the police service's role as a protector of the public. The other narrative principle is to tell a story, rather than simply trying to refute what terrorists are saying. Policymakers, advocates, and journalists frequently rely on this principle because they know that personal stories can humanize a situation and make potentially dull discussions of policy issues colorful and interesting. Personal stories may resonate because they are engaging, immediate, and intelligent. For people unused to discussing policy or unfamiliar with challenges in professions such as policing, a narrative that tells a story can help them see common human experiences.

Summary

In a world of facts, stories may be the deciding factors for people who choose between giving their support to the police or to violent extremists. Stories help individuals make sense of feelings and thoughts they have every day, give meaning to their lives, and orient their future actions. There is a competition for the hearts and minds of communities played out through individual stories that combine to create greater narratives.

Violent extremists use narratives in distinct ways to sway communities. Police need to understand violent extremist narratives before displacing them with the police's own narratives. Without this understanding, police will be ill equipped to create their own and to persuade communities to place confidence in their organization

Police face real threats from violent extremism, and they must go beyond simply countering violent extremist narratives to offer a compelling vision of how police organizations are legitimate providers of security and justice in a society. More important, they must back up any words with actions—words without actions harm credibility, sometimes fatally. Police must contend with violent extremists' verisimilitude: the likeness of truth without being true. They must instead offer actual stories based in action to displace these.

CHAPTER 3

CRAFTING NARRATIVES BASED ON ORGANIZATIONAL ASSESSMENT

DAN WADDINGTON

Executive Summary

- Extremists often create and promote messages that show police as the enemy.
- A police service's inherent weaknesses and challenges can create an environment that extremists can exploit in their efforts to propagate narratives to influence people to support the extremist cause.
- Police services that can identify, acknowledge, and address their weaknesses may improve the image of the police in the eyes of the community, thus countering the narrative of extremists.
- Countries around the world have successfully addressed police organizational and personnel issues, in turn countering negative narratives of extremists.
- An organizational assessment is necessary to understand and address institutional weaknesses. A proven methodology for organizational assessment is a SWOT (strengths, weaknesses, opportunities, threats) analysis.

Introduction

Narratives are critical to the recruitment and radicalization success of extremists. Ideas and narratives that legitimize terrorism and foster its appeal are used to rationalize violence and recruit new devotees. Many terrorists and violent extremists effectively tailor, package, and disseminate narratives in a way that reaches and resonates with individuals and groups targeted for radicalization and recruitment.[11]

Counter-terrorism strategic communications efforts must use communicative tools and construct narratives to counter messages publicized by extremists. Although there are some legitimate concerns about government use of "targeted communications," the world is full of public relations and strategic communication campaigns. It is both appropriate and advisable to make use of the power of strategic communications.

Because police officers are typically the most visible and most frequently encountered representatives of the government, local citizens often base their perceptions of the government on their attitudes toward their police service. Too often, inherent weaknesses and unaddressed challenges of a police service and its personnel create an environment that extremists can capitalize on. One standard extremist methodology is to demonize the police by creating and promoting messages that show them as the enemy. The extremist message may be fabricated, exaggerated, or based on actual weaknesses or shortcomings of the police organization and on a community's perception of the lack of service or poor response from the police organization, apathy among police officers, or police corruption and brutality. In the effort to counter extremist narratives, a positive image of the police is essential.

Police services that can identify, acknowledge, and address institutional weaknesses can improve the image of the police in the eyes of the community, thereby undermining negative narratives that beleaguer police services around the world. This chapter begins by providing two examples of police services that have recognized their weaknesses, addressed them,

---

[1] Organization for Security and Co-operation in Europe (OSCE), *Preventing Terrorism and Countering Violent Extremism and Radicalization that Lead to Terrorism: A Community-Policing Approach* (Vienna: OSCE, 2014).

and subsequently improved the way that the general public sees the police. In both cases, the services recognized specific behaviors that were undermining their relationship with the community.

The chapter then turns to the subject of organizational assessment. Before any police service starts to develop a narrative, it must first assess its strengths and weaknesses; a SWOT analysis is an effective way to accomplish this task.

Stop and Search in Spain

Stop-and-search powers provide fodder for an antipolice narrative in Spain. ("Stop and search" refers to the police power to stop, question, and search a person who is suspected of doing something illegal, such as carrying illegal drugs.) Police services often have stop-and-search powers, some of which do not require that the person be suspected of any involvement in a crime. These powers are controversial and have been criticized, in particular because of concerns about the disproportionate use of the powers against members of minority groups. The use of stop-and-search powers based on discriminatory ethnic profiling can have corrosive effects on community confidence in police. In turn, this lack of confidence can reinforce or corroborate narratives that portray police as stigmatizing and acting against members of particular national, ethnic, or religious groups.

One method used to encourage transparency and counter a negative narrative is to require detailed recording of statistics relating to the use of these powers. Another is to issue guidance and provide training to police officers to ensure that their decisions to stop and search people are based on objective criteria rather than on suspicions based on discriminatory stereotypes linked, for example, to age or membership in a minority group. These methods should be coupled with systems of external and internal oversight, and with efforts to inform people of their rights in such circumstances.

In 2007, the local police in Fuenlabrada, a city near the Spanish capital of Madrid, in cooperation with the Open Society Institute, introduced a pilot project to monitor the use of stop-and-search powers. Police officers were required to fill out a form describing the ethnicity and/or nationality of the person stopped; the name of the responsible officer; the time, date, and place of the stop; the legal grounds for the stop; the grounds for suspicion; and the outcome. (The form also provided space for officers to describe the stop situation for intelligence purposes.) The officer had to give a copy of the filled-out form to the person stopped. The form included information on an individual's rights and on how to make a complaint if the person was dissatisfied with his or her treatment by the police. The forms were reviewed by supervisors to monitor the extent of ethnic profiling.

The Open Society Institute observed that after six months of using the forms, the police had reduced the rate at which they stopped people of immigrant origin. Furthermore, the total number of stops had fallen by more than half, while the percentage of stops that led to questioning and/or charges had almost tripled. The practice of filling out the forms had led police officers to focus on their treatment of people during stops. By gathering the data and making better use of it, the Fuenlabrada police became more efficient: they made fewer stops, but the stops were more effective.[22]

This project was an effort by the police to change the narrative that they were using stop-and-search authority in an inappropriate, biased way. Ultimately, the persuasiveness of a message depends on the sender's credibility. To be successful in a campaign to counter the narratives of extremists, government institutions, including police services, must make every effort to be perceived as trustworthy and credible. The Fuenlabrada police service used documentation and data to validate its efforts, thereby gaining credibility in the eyes of the community.

An Emphasis on Community Policing in Northern Ireland

The conflict in Northern Ireland has been characterized by tensions between two communities, Protestants and Catholics, as well by as the continued use of, and support for, terrorist tactics by some individuals and groups. A lack of trust in the police service and other state institutions

---

[2] Rachel Neild and Lee Bridges, *Reducing Ethnic Profiling in the European Union: A Handbook of Good Practices* (New York: Open Society Foundations, 2012).

contributed to the conflict. Police reform has been an important part of the peace process that led to the Good Friday Agreement of 1997 and the subsequent transition to a more peaceful society. The case of Northern Ireland illustrates how the introduction of community policing within a framework based on respect for human rights and the rule of law can be part of a holistic strategy to counter antipolice narratives and strengthen public confidence in the police.

Police reform has been implemented in many ways:

- A temporary program intended to increase confidence in the police service among the Catholic community reserved 50 percent of new police officer posts for individuals from a perceived Catholic background in order to raise their numbers to 30 percent of the police service.
- Police officers working in community roles were kept in their posts for longer periods of time than in that past so that they had time to develop and maintain community relationships.
- All police work is now carried out with an eye toward community support, with an emphasis on the concept that all police officers are ultimately responsible for the protection of both communities.
- Regular meetings are held with community members to listen to concerns and provide information.
- The police service focuses on issues of particular concern to the community (e.g., controlling sex offenders and maintaining public order).

These measures assisted in countering narratives that portray the police service as existing solely to reinforce state authority.[33]

---

[3] P. Nolan, *The Northern Ireland Peace Monitoring Report,* no. 1 (Belfast: Northern Ireland Community Relations Council, 2012).

Conduct an Organizational Assessment

How do police services develop a reliable understanding of their weaknesses or shortcomings and how these might contribute to negative narratives promoted by extremists? What can and should be done to address those weaknesses and shortcomings in efforts to counter these narratives?

Understanding that the police organization must improve its image with the public to counter extremist narratives is the first step in changing the narrative. It is like knowing where you want to go on a map. You cannot know how to get where you want to go unless you know where you are. Once you know where you are and where you want to get to, you can develop directions to get there.

For an organization to know where it is, it must conduct an organizational assessment. An organizational assessment is a systematic process of obtaining valid information about the performance of the organization and the factors that affect performance. It is conducted to demonstrate areas of competence, areas for improvement, and possible risks.

There are two fundamental aspects of an organizational assessment: internal elements and external elements. Internal elements are part of the organization—its operations, structure, responsibilities, activities, and so forth. External elements do not fall directly within the agency's organizational makeup, but the organization has responsibility and accountability for them. External factors and entities may have positive or negative influence on the organization.

Examples of internal elements and external elements are presented in table 3.1. Each agency must consider all elements that could play a role in better community understanding of the organization and its environment and could therefor assist in changing narratives.

Table 3.1. Internal and external elements

Internal	**External**
• Policies and procedures	• Community problems/crimes
• Policing practices	• Community concerns
• Organizational structure	• Community attitudes
• Personnel resources	• Narratives related to the police
• Logistical resources	• External organizations

Although specific elements of an assessment will vary from one police service to another, there is little variation around factors that refer to resources, procedures, and crimes committed and reported. It can be a daunting task to compile and assess these elements, and a number of tools have been developed make the process more methodical and effective. SWOT (Strengths, Weaknesses, Opportunities, and Threats) analysis is one such tool and is used by organizations and businesses around the world as a framework to assemble, arrange, and assess their internal and external elements.

SWOT

A SWOT analysis is an organizational assessment of internal strengths and weaknesses and external opportunities and threats. It focuses on opposition variables—strength versus weaknesses and opportunities versus threats.[4] The use of SWOT analysis has been substantiated by academic peer-reviewed literature, and research supports SWOT analysis as a tool for business planning purposes across a variety of industries and interests.[5] A SWOT analysis is recommended for organizations as they begin to craft strategic alternatives.[6] Although initially developed as a tool for private

---

[4] V. Y. Tsvetkov, "Opposition Variables as a Tool of Qualitative Analysis," *World Applied Sciences Journal* 30, no. 11 (2014): 1703–1706.

[5] M. M. Helms and J. Nixon, "Exploring SWOT Analysis—Where Are We Now? A Review of Academic Research from the Last Decade," *Journal of Strategy and Management* 3, no. 3 (2010): 215–251, doi:10.1108/17554251011064837.

[6] E. H. Kessler, *SWOT Analysis Framework* (Thousand Oaks, CA: Sage, 2013).

sector business ventures, SWOT is increasingly promoted as a tool for decision making in the public sector.[77]

The SWOT approach has proven valuable specifically in assessing the viability of methodologies to counter violent extremism. In *Preventing Terrorism and Countering Violent Extremism and Radicalization that Lead to Terrorism: A Community-Policing Approach,* the Organization for Security and Co-operation in Europe (OSCE) suggests that a SWOT analysis be used as part of a situational assessment for incorporating community policing as part of a broader effort to counter violent extremism.[88] In a quantitative assessment of violence in Nigeria, Patricia Taft and Nate Haken recommend that a comprehensive qualitative assessment be conducted.[99] Referencing their collection, coding, and analysis of conflict data in Nigeria, Taft and Haken note that although their research shed light on patterns of violence and conflict, it did little to clarify the causes of, or solutions to, those conflict patterns. They suggest that a SWOT analysis would be a viable way of identifying causes and possible solutions.

SWOT analysis involves the collection of information about internal and external factors that have, or that may have, an impact on an organization.[1010] Ralph Stacey describes a SWOT analysis as a list of an organization's strengths and weaknesses as indicated by an analysis of its resources and capabilities, as well as a list of the threats and opportunities that an analysis of its environment identifies.[1111] Strategic logic requires that the future pattern of actions to be taken matches strengths with opportunities, wards off threats, and seeks to overcome weaknesses. A SWOT analysis is well-suited for assessing where an organization is and for giving it a basic sense of direction regarding where it needs to go and how to get there.

---

[7] M. Prowle, *The Changing Public Sector: A Practical Management Guide* (New York: CRC, 2016).

[8] OSCE, *Preventing Terrorism.*

[9] P. Taft and N. Haken, *Violence in Nigeria: Patterns and Trendss* (New York: Springer, 2015).

[10] D. W. Pickton and S. Wright, "What's SWOT in Strategic Analysis?" *Strategic Change* 7, no. 2 (1998): 101–109.

[11] R. D. Stacey, *Strategic Management and Organisational Dynamics: The Challenge of Complexity to Ways of Thinking about Organisations* (Harrow, UK: Pearson, 2007).

A SWOT analysis offers five key benefits as a tool for organizational assessment:

- It is simple in principle and practical to use.
- It is easy to understand.
- It focuses on the key internal and external factors affecting the organization.
- It helps identify future goals and objectives.
- It initiates further analysis.

A SWOT analysis is best illustrated as a matrix (see figure 3.2), with positive/negative and external/internal elements.

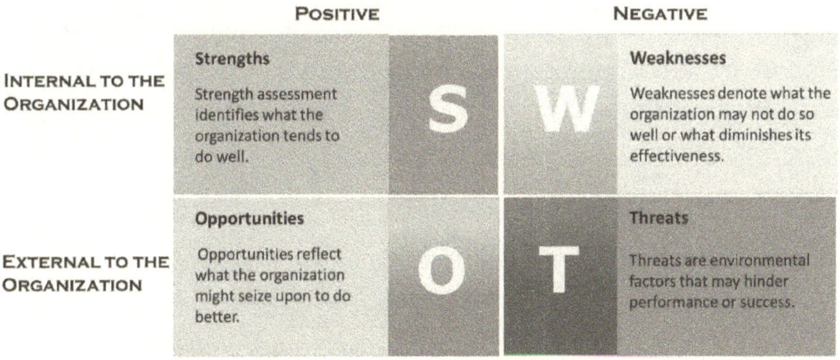

Figure 3.2. The SWOT matrix

When conducting a SWOT analysis, many police organizations make the mistake of confusing strengths with opportunities and weaknesses with threats. However, the difference is straightforward: strengths and weaknesses refer to the positive and negative aspects of the organization's internal capabilities and resources, whereas opportunities and threats refer to external influences and factors that may affect the organization. Another way to look at this in the context of creating positive narratives to counter extremist narratives is that positive aspects refer to forces helpful to establishing encouraging narratives regarding the police, whereas negative aspects are those that are hurtful to establishing such narratives.

These important distinctions help to guide what an organization can and should do to adjust course to meet desired objectives. If we adopt the same analogy illustrated in figure earlier: You can control how fast you drive and perhaps even what type of vehicle you use. You can decide which roads and turns to take to get you to your destination. However, you do not necessarily have the option of using roads that are closed or blocked.

It is important that objectivity be maintained throughout a SWOT analysis, rather than basing the analysis on individual perceptions. Data need to be gathered from numerous sources, both internal and external, to support the analysis. Data should relate to the issue at hand, in this case the ability of the police organization to create positive narratives. Internal data could be drawn from elements in table 3.1 (e.g., policies and procedures, current police practices, organizational structure, and personnel and logistical resources) and could include operational and statistical reports. External data could also be drawn from elements suggested in table 3.1 (e.g., surveys identifying community perceptions of the police and crime) but they should also come from external sources such as government reports, news outlets, and social media.

How to Conduct a SWOT Analysis

Create a Team to Conduct the Analysis

The first step of a SWOT analysis is to put together a team able to conduct the analysis effectively. The SWOT team should consist of open-minded, knowledgeable representatives from both the police service and the community. Police team members should include midlevel managers or even high-level commanders, employees from throughout the agency, and frontline supervisors. The same considerations should determine the selection of representatives from the community: they should be business leaders and high-level community activists, as well as individuals who are committed to working with the police in a positive way to make improvements. The team should be relatively small, ten people or fewer, to keep the process efficient.

The following considerations should be borne in mind prior to starting a SWOT analysis:

- A SWOT analysis is subjective. It is not an exact science, but using both quantitative and qualitative objective data helps users trust the data and the process.
- Keep the SWOT simple. Avoid complexity—pick out issues on which the organization needs to concentrate its efforts. After addressing those issues, if other issues continue to be problematic, do another SWOT analysis to address those other issues.
- Be realistic about the organization's strengths and weaknesses. Ask for input from employees and leaders, and then use it in the analysis.
- Use the SWOT analysis to distinguish between where the organization is now and where it wants to be in the future.
- Be specific. Stay focused on the topic at hand—namely, creating a positive narrative.
- Apply the SWOT analysis in terms of the organization's "competition." While conducting the SWOT analysis, consider who creates the negative narrative and how it can be addressed.

Teams performing a SWOT analysis should develop ground rules that define how to conduct team meetings. Ground rules help promote efficiency and participation. Some helpful meeting ground rules include the following:

- Respect one another and refrain from making personal attacks.
- Acknowledge that it is acceptable to disagree.
- Listen to others; do not interrupt.
- Everyone participates; no one dominates; value the diversity of team members.
- Recognize that all ideas are potentially good ideas; do not rush to evaluate suggestions; keep an open mind.
- Stick to the agenda—stay on task.
- Respect confidentiality: what is said in the meeting should stay in the meeting.

With a team in place, the analysis can begin. Figure 3.3 illustrates the general flow of the SWOT process.

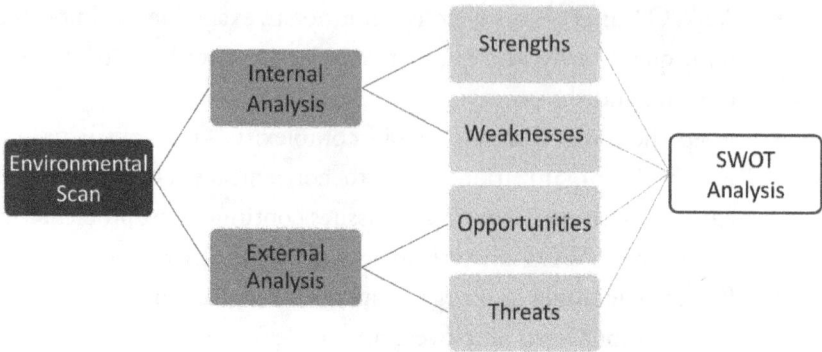

Figure 3.3. The SWOT process

Perform an Environmental Scan

The environmental scan is a data- and information-gathering phase that provides the analytical elements needed for a SWOT analysis. In the environmental scan, the goal is to accumulate as much data and information about the organization and its environment as possible. You will be more successful if you segregate data and information gathering into two general areas: internal and external. Look for information related to the organization and its environment that might undermine negative narratives promoted by extremists and help generate positive ones. The types of information that can be valuable include the following:

Internal

- People (human resources)
  o People and skills
  o Current training curricula
- Current policies and established procedures
- Processes
  o Financial resources
  o Governance
  o Management/leadership

- o Personnel development
- o Internal communication capabilities

External

- Demographics
- Economic data
- Political/legal
- Sociological dynamics
- Environmental issues
- Technology capabilities, including social media/web-based engagement
- Surveys
- Community mapping
- Public meetings
- Workshops and focus groups
- Forums

Having this information at your fingertips offers significant advantages in terms of knowledge, credibility, and awareness:

- *Knowledge.* Knowing the facts is a way of determining the size of the gap between where the organization is and the narratives that are being spread about the organization. Gathering information reveals the magnitude of the problem.
- *Credibility.* With data to illustrate issues, the organization comes across as knowledgeable, serious, and well organized. It shows that personnel understand and are serious about the issues.
- *Awareness.* Use data to raise community awareness of three aspects of the situation: how serious the problem is, how well (or how poorly) the community accurately understands the organization, and how well the organization has addressed the issue of improving its image and associated narratives.

With data and information in hand, the next stage is to assess them in the context of strengths, weaknesses, opportunities, and threats. There are four basic steps in this process:

1. *Identify strengths of the organization as they relate to changing the public narrative.* Develop a list of the internal strengths of the organization that incorporates feedback from team members, surveys, and other sources. Discuss the strengths and clarify any questions or confusion. Examples of strengths include a large organization with lots of personnel at its disposal and a strong organizational desire for change. List the strengths in the appropriate quadrant on a SWOT matrix.

2. *Identify weaknesses of the organization as they relate to changing the public narrative.* Generate a list of the agency's weaknesses. Weaknesses are internal factors that may impact narratives related to the police negatively. Examples of weaknesses could include the absence of procedural manuals and the lack of an employee-mentoring program. However, what is perceived as a strength in one regard could in reality be a weakness of the organization. For example, a large organization may be seen as a strength because large organizations tend to have a lot of personnel resources. However, if it is not only large but also autocratic, the organization will limit decision making by patrol officers, making it difficult for them to engage effectively with the public and thus undermining community policing efforts. Another weakness of a large organization is that it tends to resist change, just as a large battleship cannot change course easily. List weaknesses in the appropriate quadrant on the matrix.

3. *Identify opportunities to change the public narrative.* Opportunities are external factors, as opposed to the internal factors of strengths and weaknesses. Opportunities could include new relevant training programs from international donors or a diverse workforce that is available to the police service. List opportunities in the appropriate quadrant on the matrix.

4. *Identify potential threats to the organization as they relate to changing the public narrative.* Threats are also external factors. Threats could have a negative impact on organizational efforts and could include a projected increase in the cost of employee health insurance or an expected reduction in government funding. An opportunity may also be perceived as a threat. For example, new technology tools might be an opportunity, but they may also threaten staffing levels. List threats in the appropriate quadrant on the matrix.

During the analysis, good practices suggest that working with one quadrant of the matrix at a time helps keep the team on task and on time. Many teams find it helpful to set time limits for discussion, as well as ground rules, so that the group does not circle around a topic endlessly. Working with one quadrant at a time, the team should develop a list of all the factors in that quadrant. For example, starting with strengths, the team can list all internal strengths of the police service, using its own drafted matrices, feedback from employees, and information gathered during the environmental scan.

The team should continue in this fashion until it has brainstormed separate lists for all four quadrants. The team may find that what is considered a strength may also be considered a weakness, and a threat may also be an opportunity. If that happens, the item should appear on both lists.

Table 3.2 presents a sample SWOT matrix. Note that each point is numbered in its respective quadrant (i.e., point 1 under strengths is "S1"; point 2 under weaknesses is "W2"). This allows for easy reference later.

Table 3.2. Sample SWOT matrix[12]

HELPFUL (INTERNAL) to establishing encouraging narratives	HURTFUL (INTERNAL) to establishing encouraging narratives
STRENGTHS	WEAKNESSES
S1. Police officials and commissioned officers have been receptive and responsive to new policing philosophies.	W1. The police organization is very large and unwieldy.
S2. Community engagement principles have been positively received by police officers and executives.	W2. The organization has historically had a militaristic focus and relied primarily on tactical/kinetic responses.
S3. The police have demonstrated the ability and willingness to evolve into a more community-focused organization.	W3. There have been publicized incidents of police corruption.
	W4. There have been publicized incidents of police brutality.
S4. The organization is large, with a lot of personnel resources.	W5. The organization is very autocratic and top-down; there is no decision-making authority at the line level.
	W6. There is institutional resistance to change.

---

[12] Waddington, D. (2017) A SWOT Analysis of Community Policing as a Reform Schema For the Egyptian National Police To Counter Violent Extremism. University at Albany, Albany, New York

HELPFUL (EXTERNAL) to establishing encouraging narratives	HURTFUL (EXTERNAL) to establishing encouraging narratives
OPPORTUNITIES	THREATS
O1. When police services focus on improving relations with the public, they undermine the negative narrative that police are the "enemy."	T1. There is a history of distrust in the police that is not easily erased.
	T2. Successful measurable police reform has proven to be difficult to achieve throughout the world.
O2. International support and training are available to help the police organization transition to be more community focused.	
	T3. Community engagement takes a long time to implement.
O3. Community policing continues to be the preferred model for international police reform. Community policing has been proven to improve the image of the police.	T4. It takes a lot of resources to effectively engage the community.
	T5. Community policing and similar community engagement programs require autonomy and self-initiation for police in the field.
O4. Police can take advantage of social media networks to challenge negative narratives.	
	T6. There is a well-established media campaign against the police.

A comprehensive analysis would likely uncover many more issues than are listed in table 3.2, which is a simple example to demonstrate the process. When strengths, weaknesses, opportunities, and threats are consolidated in a SWOT analysis, a clear picture is provided as to where the organization stands. The output of the SWOT analysis is not simply a matrix or grid; that matrix should be part of a longer but nonetheless concise report that assists in establishing meaningful, realistic goals and activities.

An initial review of the SWOT matrix in table 3.2 indicates that there are more weaknesses and threats than there are strengths and opportunities. Some weaknesses, especially those with greater impact, may hinder the efforts of the police in creating positive narratives about their service. The organization's administrative/analytical team should consider each element of the SWOT analysis and ask the following questions:

- How can we use our strengths to take advantage of (or seize) the opportunities?
- How can we overcome (or eradicate) our weaknesses by taking advantage of the opportunities?
- How can we use our strengths to avoid (or negate) the threats?
- How can we minimize our weaknesses and avoid the threats?

As organizations answer these questions, they will begin to understand the internal and external forces they contend with and how to address them. Each organization should use this understanding to develop a plan of action designed to shape the organization's the strategic development as it relates to changing the public narrative.

For example, in table 3.2, S3 is "The police have demonstrated the ability and willingness to evolve into a more community-focused organization." This ability could be significant in helping to address one of the listed weaknesses, W2, "The organization has historically had a militaristic focus and relied primarily on tactical/kinetic responses." O4, "Police can take advantage of social media networks to challenge negative narratives," could be a means to address T6, "There is a well-established media campaign against the police."

The SWOT analysis is about capitalizing on strengths, overcoming weaknesses, taking advantage of opportunities, and countering threats. It is also about identifying the most important organizational issues, setting priorities to address them, appraising the options, and taking action. To counter extremism, the SWOT analysis should be conducted in the context of organizational narratives and the community.

Summary

An honest, systematic self-assessment can help a police organization change a negative narrative. The organization should consider publicizing the SWOT matrix or publishing a summary of the assessment process and findings along with a plan to minimize weaknesses and threats and enhance strengths and weaknesses; such openness, self-criticism, and commitment to improvement can go a long way in improving the public's perception of the police. It shows that the police service is making strides in changing its image. Ultimately, this can help invalidate the kind of negative narratives about police typically promoted by extremist groups.

The analytical process described here can provide guidance and recommendations about how to design and prioritize police reform efforts in order to change the broader narrative about the police. Police reform is a difficult and challenging process. Reform programs must be attuned to the local context and require comprehensive organizational assessments such as the one presented here if they are to be successful. SWOT can be a simple and effective tool, provided it is not used as a response. It is intended to be used as a summary tool for self-assessment and analysis, and as a guide to organize and prioritize potential responses.

CHAPTER 4
GUIDELINES FOR DEVELOPING POSITIVE NARRATIVES

STEVAN WEINE

Executive Summary

- A step-by-step framework can guide police in developing narratives for community-oriented policing to prevent violent extremism.
- Police can use this framework to develop and deliver new narratives for community-oriented policing to prevent violent extremism.

Introduction

Police can play a leadership role in preventing violent extremism, a role that goes beyond their traditional coercive counterterrorism activities such as arresting and prosecuting. To effectively engage the public in the fight against terrorism and to kindle productive conversations about alternative approaches to violent extremism, police need to adopt a new narrative strategy for talking with the public that supplements the role of coercive counterterrorism strategies.

Elements of a Strong Narrative

To advance the current conversation on violent extremism, the police need to craft strong narratives that are based on sound narrative principles. Experts teach that every strong narrative should have at least two key elements: a classical argument and a complete narrative.

A Classical Argument

A classical argument can be used to build strong narratives concerning community-oriented policing to prevent violent extremism.[11] A classical argument provides background or context that is relevant to a specific audience. It states a claim, presents evidence clearly and emphatically, takes account of opposing viewpoints, and anticipates objections. It concludes in a satisfying and effective way. Joseph Williams and Gregory Colomb, the authors of a seminal work on narratives, articulate five questions to address in a classical argument:[22]

- What are you claiming?
- What reasons do you have for believing your claim?
- What evidence do you base those reasons on?
- What principle connects or makes your reasons relevant to your claims?
- What about potential disagreements with the claim?

Police can refer to these questions as they develop and sharpen their narratives regarding community-oriented policing to prevent violent extremism.

---

[1] Walter Beale, *Real Writing: Argumentation, Reflection, Information with Stylistic Options* (Glenview, IL: Scott Foresman, 1982).

[2] Joseph Williams and Gregory Colomb, *Style: Lessons in Clarity and Grace* (New York: Longman, 2001).

Police who are building narratives on community-oriented policing to prevent violent extremism also need to present a complete narrative so that community members can productively consider and engage with specific changes from the traditional approaches to terrorism in the criminal justice system.[33] A complete narrative asks and answers a broad range of questions. Police should always try to address the following four questions as part of a complete narrative about terrorism and its impact:

- Why does terrorism matter to society?
- How does coercive counterterrorism work and why is it not sufficient to defeat terrorism?
- What else needs to be done to improve public safety concerning terrorism?
- Why are community-oriented practices necessary for preventing terrorism?

The framework presented in this chapter (which is based on empirical data concerning narrative approaches to criminal justice reform) suggests specific ways that these four questions should be addressed.[44]

Answering these four questions will involve generating narratives that do the work of explaining multiple key components such as core values, how counterterrorism works, how alternatives to counterterrorism work, how core police functions protect the community from violence, and how core police functions build community resilience.

Other questions to consider will be articulated in the following framework.

---

[3] M. O'Neil, N. Kendall-Taylor, and A. Volmert, "New Narratives: Changing the Frame on Crime and Justice," a Frame Works Message Memo (Washington, DC: Frame Works Institute, 2016), https://docplayer.net/33391313-New-narratives-changing-the-frame-on-crime-and-justice.html.

[4] Ibid.

A Step-by-Step Framework for Building Community-Oriented Policing Narratives

With these principles in mind, consider the framework for building community-oriented policing narratives presented in table 4.1.

Table 4.1. A framework for building community-oriented policing narratives [5]

- Step 1: Clarify what CVE objective(s) you wish to accomplish
- Step 2: Identify and acknowledge the community or communities of interest and engage with stakeholders
- Step 3: Listen and analyze how your objective(s) relate to community needs, strengths, and priorities
- Step 4: Draft a community-oriented policing narrative that includes one of more of the following components:
    - o   Step 4a: Explain core values, how countering terrorism works, and alternative solutions
    - o   Step 4b: Explain core police functions for protecting the community from violence
    - o   Step 4c: Explain core police functions for building community resilience
- Step 5: Identify specific narrative practices to be used to reach the target audiences
- Step 6: Develop a plan for quality improvement and monitoring and evaluation of the narratives

---

[5] Hedayah has developed a 9-step framework for Development of Counter-Narratives that is available in three regional collections South East Asia, Middle East and North Africa and East Africa. available on Hedayah's website under publications: http://www.hedayahcenter.org/publications/89/report

Step 1: Clarify CVE Objectives

To clarify CVE objectives, police first need to draw upon a new framework that comes, not from within the field of criminal justice, but from the field of public health prevention.

Public health prevention encompasses primary, secondary, and tertiary levels of prevention. Prevention in public health consists of activities that protect people from actual or potential threats to health and their health consequences. Seen from a public health perspective, everything CVE programs do involves some level of prevention (see figure 4.1).

Figure 4.1. Three-tiered model of public health prevention as applied to the prevention of violent extremism.

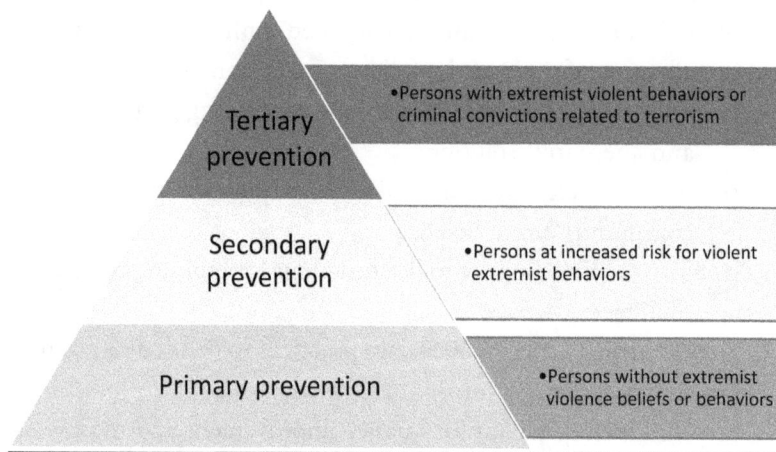

Source: Adapted from S. Weine, D. Eisenman, C. Polutnik, J. Kinnsler, and D. Glik, "Addressing Violent Extremism as Public Health Policy and Practice," *Behavioral Sciences of Terrorism and Political Aggression* (2016): 1–14.

In public health, primary prevention aims to protect whole populations against exposure to risk factors that lead to injury. In CVE, primary prevention targets the whole community, the vast majority of whom do not have problematic behaviors associated with violent extremism, through activities such as community-wide counter-messaging campaigns that aim to shift cultural norms.

Secondary prevention in public health targets individuals considered at higher risk for acquiring a given condition. Secondary prevention in CVE focuses on persons considered "at risk" for violent behaviors, such as individuals who have been identified with behaviors or communications that signal they are at risk of committing violence but have not yet committed a violent extremist act.[66]

Tertiary prevention is aimed at persons who already have the health condition and is intended to improve their outcomes. In CVE, tertiary prevention is aimed at those with demonstrated violent behavior or association with a terrorist organization. In regard to CVE, tertiary prevention could mean rehabilitating and reintegrating persons who have manifested criminal, violent extremist behaviors, such as returned foreign fighters.

In developing a narrative about community-oriented practices to prevent violent extremism, the first step police need to take is to clarify the CVE objectives of the activities that they are conducting. One way to do this is explain how their activities are linked to goals for each of the three prevention levels. The police's narrative should also emphasize that, like public health programs, its CVE programming is rooted in civil society ownership, community collaboration, broader prevention programming, and non-securitized approaches

Step 2: Identify and Acknowledge the Community or Communities of Interest and Engage with Stakeholders

Police need to identify the community or communities with whom they are working to achieve CVE goals. Thought should be given to how the police can best define the community and demonstrate that they understand the community context. All communication should make it clear that the police understand the difference between viewing the community as an information source versus involving it in the problem-solving process.

---

6 S. Weine and J. Cohen, *Moving Beyond Motive-Based Categories of Targeted Violence* (Argonne, IL: Argonne National Laboratory, U.S. Department of Energy, 2015).

Community-oriented policing relies on the latter approach. Central to community-oriented policing is the concept that police meet with community stakeholders and document community members' experiences, perceptions, and understanding of terrorism, the police, and community-oriented policing practices. All these dimensions should find their way into the narratives.

Step 3: Analyze How CVE Objectives Relate to Community Needs, Strengths, and Priorities

Police narratives around community-oriented policing must incorporate and be responsive to community needs, strengths, and priorities. The narratives should communicate an accurate and deep understanding of the community within which the police hope to intervene, including recognition of the dominant narratives that community members have of their overall needs, strengths, and priorities. Police should also recognize the dominant narratives that community members have of the police and police activities to combat terrorism and other forms of political violence. Police often need to create a narrative that is an alternative to the community's dominant narrative, such as emphasizing bases for trust as opposed to causes of distrust.

Step 4: Draft a Community-Oriented Policing Narrative

Step 4a: Explain Core Values, How Countering Terrorism Works, and Alternative Solutions. The community-oriented policing narrative should identify and explain the core values embodied in the effort to address terrorism through alternative solutions that involve community practices associated with CVE. The core values establish why society must address issues related to terrorism and counterterrorism. Police can use metaphors to explain how CVE works and the need for alternatives to coercive counterterrorism.

Three core values that have been used to argue for criminal justice reform may be employed in community-oriented policing narratives:[78]

- *National progress:* Convey the urgency of the problem and advance the belief that meaningful change is both possible and desirable.
- *Human potential:* Orient people toward community strategies and build support for initiatives that prevent violence.
- *Problem-solving value:* Orient people to the importance of moving away from surveillance, arrest, and prosecution as the exclusive function and goals of counterterrorism.

Police should identify one or more of these values. If other core values seem pertinent to explaining the need for community practices, particularly values that pertain to the local sociocultural context, then these should be used in addition to or instead of the ones listed here.

Explanatory metaphors can be used to explain the core concepts of counterterrorism. Metaphors are linguistic devices that help people think and talk about a complex concept in new ways. They work by comparing an abstract or unfamiliar idea to something concrete and familiar. They can create space for productive thinking and discussion.

One example of an explanatory metaphor is the Whack-a-Mole game. This game illustrates the practice of repeatedly getting rid of something only to have it reappear. The Whack-a-Mole metaphor can be used to illustrate how coercive counterterrorism strategies repeatedly attempt to get rid of terrorism, only to see it keep reappearing.

Another useful metaphor is the mosquito. When we discover a mosquito biting us, our reaction is to swat it. But does this action discourage other mosquitos from biting us? No. To avoid getting bitten by mosquitos, we need to close the window and doors or protect ourselves with netting or repellant.

Yet another metaphor is that of bicycle gears. Just like we need different gears for cycling up and down hills, counterterrorism needs different solutions for different situations. When we rely on use of force as our only gear, we lose the ability to match the right solution to a specific problem. We get stuck with incomplete approaches to dealing with terrorism and

---

[7] O'Neil, Kendall-Taylor, and Volmert, "New Narratives."

improving public safety. We all know it is hard to get to where you need to go if you only have one gear to use. Counterterrorism works the same way. It cannot do the things that we expect of it—make our society better and safer—if it has only one approach. We need different gears if we are to address, prevent, and reduce terrorism effectively. And we need alternatives to surveillance and arrest—such as better mental health treatment—if we want to improve public safety.

Police officers should consider how metaphors might work in their communities. What other metaphors reflect the limitations of coercive counterterrorism and the need for community strategies? What other metaphors reflect solutions for public safety with respect to terrorism? Police should be encouraged to draw from the local culture and language to identify the most appropriate explanatory metaphors for illustrating alternative solutions to addressing terrorism.

Step 4b: Explain Core Police Functions for Protecting Communities from Violence. The narrative of community-oriented practices should anchor the approach to violent extremism within the broader landscape of how police protect communities from other forms of violence, especially targeted violence.[89] It should also explain what community policing is and why police use community policing. Explaining community policing should involve defining and operationalizing the community policing practices of engaging, building trust, educating, problem solving, mobilizing, and other relevant practices. For example, a study of the Los Angeles Police Department identified the following practices being used by the department in its community policing approach to counter violence extremism:[910]

- *Engage:* Community outreach officers meet and establish one-on-one relationships with community leaders that open communication channels. They build partnerships with community-based organizations, including faith-based and interfaith organizations.

---

8 Weine and Cohen, *Moving Beyond Motive-Based Categories.*
9 Stevan Weine, Ahmed Younis, and Chloe Polutnik, "Community Policing to Counter Violent Extremism: A Process Evaluation in Los Angeles," Final Report, Office of University Programs, Science and Technology Directorate, U.S. Department of Homeland Security (College Park, MD: START, 2017).

- *Build trust:* Community outreach officers establish honest and open dialogue on sensitive issues such as terrorism, hate crimes, and discrimination with community leaders and members. They acknowledge and promote mutual understanding of communities' historical traumas and their present needs and strengths. The police department aims to be as transparent as possible regarding crime fighting and police conduct.
- *Educate:* Community outreach officers teach communities about crime (including hate crimes), police work, and community resources to combat criminal activity. This includes building knowledge and awareness in communities about violent extremism and how to prevent it.
- *Problem solve:* Community outreach officers help communities and individuals respond to their current problems. This includes helping communities respond appropriately to Islamophobia, discrimination, and hate speech and crimes. Officers also help community members access resources to address social, legal, and mental and physical health concerns. They assist immigrants and refugees in promoting their integration and addressing their security concerns. They provide communities with knowledge and skills to assess the threat level of individuals and educate them on how to respond.
- *Mobilize*: Community outreach officers promote the civic engagement of community members, including promoting advocacy by women and youth on civic and public safety issues. They provide community-based organizations with consultation, materials, information, and support on how to build resilience to violent extremism.

Step 4c: Explain Core Police Functions for Building Community Resilience. The community-oriented policing narrative should explain what community resilience is and why it so important in the battle against violent extremism. It should make clear how police actions can build community resilience and how the police protect against violent extremism by promoting community resilience.

Community resilience has been defined as the sustained ability of a community to utilize available resources to respond to, withstand, and recover from adverse situations. According to Fran Norris, a community psychologist, four primary sets of resources underlie community resilience: economic development, social capital, information and communication, and community competence.[10][11]

Research conducted among the Somali-American community in the U.S. metropolitan area of Minneapolis-St. Paul looked at community resilience to violence extremism.[11][12] The researchers identified forty-three protective resources that mitigated against thirty-seven risk factors. These resources were organized into the DOVE (Diminishing Opportunities for Violent Extremism) model, which explains how multiple risk factors combine to create opportunities for entering into violent extremism and how protective resources can stop, delay, or diminish such opportunities. It proposes that prevention programming be directed at three major risk factors: unaccountable times and unobserved spaces for youth; the perceived social legitimacy of violent extremism; and the potential for contact with terrorist recruiters or associates. Examples of specific components of community resilience include parental monitoring and supervision; family confidantes; family social support; family involvement in education; access to services and helpers; trusted accurate information sources; increased activities in supervised community spaces; mentoring of youth, and increased civilian liaisons to police.

Police officers who are constructing narratives of community resilience should consider including some the components mentioned above or identify others that may be particular to their context so as to give their narratives some specificity beyond the abstract notion of community resilience. This is not meant to be a definitive list, however. Police officers should also ask themselves what other elements of community resilience community members might identify.

---

[10] F. H. Norris, S.P. Stevens, B. Pfefferbaum K. F. Wyche, and R.L. Pfefferbaum, "Community Resilience as a Metaphor, Theory, Set of Capacities, and Strategy for Disaster Readiness," *American Journal of Community Psychology* 41 (2008): 127–150.

[11] S. M. Weine and O. Ahmed, *Building Resilience to Violent Extremisms among Somali-Americans in Minneapolis-St. Paul,* Final Report to Human Factors/ Behavioral Sciences Division, Science and Technology Directorate, U.S. Department of Homeland Security (College Park, MD: START, 2012).

The process of creating resilience narratives starts with the police but it must include the communities being served and should lead to the creation of shared narratives. Work toward a narrative should begin with gathering dominant "stories" from major stakeholders—where do they see risks and dangers? who needs protection? who are the main characters? what are the key motifs and themes of the existing narratives?—and continue to find points of intersection and potential alignment with the evolving narrative of community resilience.

Step 5: Identify Practices to Reach Target Audiences

In addition to developing community-oriented policing narratives, the police need to draw on standard practices in public relations and be mindful of how the narrative can best be delivered. Steps in this effort include:

- Identify the intended audience
- Choose the medium of communication
- Choose credible messengers
- Use the Internet and social media
- Reach out to pertinent subgroups such as youth and parents
- Invite community members to collaborate in shaping the messaging

Step 6: Develop a Plan for Quality Improvement and Monitoring and Evaluation of Community-Oriented Policing Narratives

The development and delivery of community policing narratives should be subject to monitoring and evaluation that seeks to learn from experience and improve quality over time. It should incorporate one or more of the following approaches:

- *Examine the narratives:* Use narrative or qualitative analysis to determine what is in the narratives.[12][13]

---

[12] K. Charmaz, *Constructing Grounded Theory: A Practical Guide Through Qualitative Analysis* (London: Sage, 2006).

- *Examine the processes:* Determine how the narratives were developed, delivered, and received utilizing process evaluation or implementation evaluation methods.[1314]
- *Examine the impact:* Use impact evaluation methods to determine the impact of the narratives and determine whether or not the delivery of the narratives led to changes.[1415]

Summary

Creating narratives is a key element of a community policing approach to preventing terrorism. There are four basic principles to follow when creating a narrative:

- Tell a complete narrative.
- Begin with one or more of three core values: national progress, human potential, and problem solving.
- Use metaphors. For example, the Whack-a-Mole metaphor demonstrates how coercive counterterrorism strategies repeatedly try to get rid of terrorism, only to see it reappear; the swatting mosquitos metaphor explains how coercive counterterrorism puts us in a reactive posture; and the gears metaphor helps people think about alternative solutions involving community-oriented policing.
- Explain how community-oriented policing will enhance community resilience by strengthening economic resources, social capital, information and communication, and community competency.

Using the framework presented here, police services can develop and deliver strong alternative narratives of community-oriented policing regarding violent extremism.

---

[13] Michael Scriven, "Beyond Formative and Summative Evaluation," In *Evaluation and Education: A Quarter Century*, ed. M. W. McLaughlin and E. D. C. Phillips (Chicago: University of Chicago Press, 1991).

[14] Ibid.

CHAPTER 5

BRINGING NARRATIVES HOME: MESSAGING DIRECTLY TO AUDIENCES IN YOUR NETWORK

TALENE BILAZARIAN

Executive Summary

- Two-way engagement between police and local communities advances community policing and CVE objectives.
- Police should engage with a broad range of groups in the community, employing narratives that foster effective partnerships for CVE.
- Police should develop connections across community networks, going beyond community leaders alone and working closely with local service providers and other groups to address violent extremism.
- Examples of police engagement with groups such as women, youth, religious leaders, and public service providers can guide police in efforts to engage with community members for CVE.

Introduction

Using narratives, police can foster more positive, collaborative relationships between themselves and communities. The role of police in CVE, the importance of narratives, and the need for narratives that address both police strengths and weaknesses have been outlined in earlier chapters. This chapter discusses how police can bring the narrative framework presented in chapter 4 directly to the smaller groups that make up the wider community. By examining research into local CVE delivery, this chapter emphasizes the importance of police engaging with the broadest possible range of groups in the community and presenting police narratives. Police need to engage with the broadest possible range of groups in the community to ensure that their narratives are understood, and their priorities are developed in line with local concerns. The chapter provides a framework for the delivery of narratives and best practices based on research on city-level CVE efforts. The examples presented here are intended to serve as guidance to empower police in varied contexts, facing unique challenges, to organize two-way engagement and communicate narratives.

Importance of Community Engagement and Narratives for CVE

Both the policy[1] and the academic[2] literature stress the importance of community participation in preventing terrorism and fighting crime. Many

---

[1] Alejandro Beutel, *Community-Led Approaches to Countering Violent Extremism in the United States* (Washington, DC: Brookings Institution, 2015), https://www. brookings.edu/blog/markaz/2015/05/30/community-led-approaches-to-countering-violent-extremism-in-the-united-states/.

[2] G. Blum and P. B. Heymann, *Laws, Outlaws, and Terrorists: Lessons from the War on Terrorism* (Cambridge, MA: MIT Press, 2010); A. K. Cronin, *How Terrorism Ends: Understanding the Decline and Demise of Terrorist Campaigns* (Princeton, NJ: Princeton University Press, 2009); S. G. Jones and M. C. Libicki, *How Terrorist Groups End: Lessons for Countering Al-Qa'ida* (Santa Monica, CA: RAND Corp., 2008); and Charles Kurzman, *Muslim-American Terrorism Since 9/11: An Accounting* (Chapel Hill, NC: Triangle Center on Terrorism and Homeland Security, February 2, 2011), http://kurzman.unc.edu/files/2011/06/Kurzman_Muslim-American_Terrorism_Since_911_An_Accounting.pdf.

communities have legitimate reason to be cautious of working closely with their local police. However, communities can be an essential partner for police, assisting them in identifying hard-to-access information that can be used to prevent terrorism. Community leaders, family members, and other local community members also can challenge extremism in noncriminal instances where police must take a less active role. Police are most effective working in partnership with communities to address crime and terrorism. By contrast, when police forces try to operate alone, they may be left guessing about risks and priorities in their community.

What drives partnerships between police and communities? What makes communities more willing to work with police in CVE efforts? There are numerous factors at work, ranging from overall levels of crime to the responsiveness of police when community members request their assistance.[3] Research highlights the importance of community trust in the police for motivating public cooperation on counterterrorism.[4] Studies show that police best maintain public trust when they use police powers

---

[3] There is debate about how communities evaluate their police and when police are considered legitimate. The authors of *Police in War* highlight several factors in this consideration, including "level of crime, behaviour of police, quickness of police response or punishing of guilty offenders." See David H. Bayley and Robert Perito, *The Police in War: Fighting Insurgency, Terrorism, and Violent Crime* (Boulder, CO: Lynne Rienner, 2010), 101.

[4] Sirpa Virta, "Community Policing Meets New Challenges," in *Policing Meets New Challenges: Preventing Radicalization and Recruitment*, ed. Sirpa Virta (Finland: University of Tampere, Department of Management Studies, 2008); Basia Spalek, "Community Policing, Trust, and Muslim Communities in Relation to 'New Terrorism,'" *Politics and Policy* 38, no. 4 (2010); and Basia Spalek, "Community Engagement for Counterterrorism in Britain: An Exploration of the Role of 'Connectors' in Countering Takfiri Jihadist Terrorism," *Studies in Conflict & Terrorism* 37, no. 10 (2014): 825–841.

fairly in their daily activities.[5] Police can strengthen their relationships with the communities they serve by combining fair and effective policing with the use of narratives in which police communicate their actions and priorities around a broader commitment to protect the community. A combination of responsive police activity, community engagement, and the use of narratives can help build public confidence in the police in the long term.

This chapter draws on unpublished research by the author on CVE implementation in US and UK cities.[6] The research compares several cities that differ in terms of the ways communities participate in local CVE efforts. In some cities, community members showed a higher level of willingness to engage with police and participate in CVE efforts. Community members helped police understand community dynamics, which informed the police's strategic activities and engagements with the community. Police relied on civil society actors to address noncriminal concerns such as social alienation or extremism, asking them to provide mentorship or religious guidance, recognizing that police are less suited to address these challenges. Local community members referenced the importance of continual engagement and consultation opportunities with the police, citing instances of police responsiveness that encouraged them to work with police on CVE initiatives. In some instances, when policing narratives were questioned or challenged, community members even defended police publicly and indicated support for how police handled violent extremism locally.

---

[5] These research findings are specific to the United Kingdom and the United States in that they focus on Muslim diaspora communities in both of these countries. See A. Huq, T. Tyler, and S. Schulhofer, "Mechanisms for Eliciting Cooperation in Counter Terrorism Policing: Evidence from the United Kingdom," *Journal of Empirical Legal Studies* 8, no. 4 (2011): 728–766; and Tom R. Tyler, Stephen Schulhofer, and Aziz Z. Huq, "Legitimacy and Deterrence Effects in Counterterrorism Policing: A Study of Muslim Americans," *Law and Society Review* 44, no. 2 (2010): 365–402.

[6] The research attempts to compare similar cities that share broadly similar terrorism threats, budgetary resources, management structures, and rates of crime. Despite these similarities, significant differences exist in the ways communities relate to their police officers around CVE programs. Out of respect for these communities and their police, city names are unidentified here.

In other cities, relations between police and communities were less collaborative. Communities avoided consulting or engaging directly with police, and police offered few opportunities for communities to meet directly with them. In these areas, community members were more reluctant to advise police about safety concerns or priorities. In effect, police in these areas worked to address crime and counter violent extremism with little insight or support from the community, producing less carefully designed CVE efforts.

The research highlights the importance of police engaging strategically with communities, which was a key part of building greater public confidence in police locally. This strategic engagement involved interfacing with key community leaders as well as a wider range of community groups and individuals, including them as partners in the problem-solving process. One way that police create long-term partnerships is by using narratives and entering into a mutual dialogue with the community. For police to ensure that their narratives resonate, they need to invest in two-way community engagement, where police and community members mutually exchange ideas about risks, priorities, and concerns to ensure effective policing. With two-way engagement, communities become partners in making security happen. Feedback from communities informs how police view their priorities and deliver services to the public.

What Is Two-Way Engagement?

Before discussing how police should use two-way engagement within their communities to advance CVE objectives, it is important to conceptualize two-way engagement. The criminologist Andy Myhill provides a useful definition for community engagement that captures the importance of the two-way component:

> The process of enabling the participation of citizens and communities in policing at their chosen level, ranging from providing information and reassurance, to empowering them to identify and implement solutions to local problems and influence strategic priorities and decisions. The police, citizens and communities must have

the willingness, capacity and opportunity to participate. The police service and partner organizations must have a responsibility to engage and, unless there is a justifiable reason, the presumption is that they must respond to community input.[7]

Two-way engagement enables the participation of citizens in policing and ensures that police are responsive to community feedback. This approach to policing broadly and CVE specifically sets a cycle in motion: police reach out to communities and get feedback from them about their concerns; this engagement helps police do their jobs better in line with local priorities; enhanced responsiveness in turn catalyzes greater public confidence in the police, heightening community willingness to support and assist police in the long term.

When police engage with communities, they should use narratives to contextualize their work, describing their commitment to protect the communities they serve and their intention to work with civilians to challenge crime and terrorism. Ultimately, however, police narratives can dissolve into propaganda if they are not combined with meaningful action, where police deliver effective community policing and respond appropriately to community concerns. The following sections outline how police can effectively combine the use of narratives with two-way engagement to build public confidence and partnerships between police and communities in CVE efforts.

Engage Broadly across the Community Network

For police to maintain the confidence of their communities, they must engage with all of the community to learn what concerns community members have about the police, thereby developing relationships across wide community networks. This collaboration helps ensure that the community as a whole and the many groups inside it—not merely select individuals—will understand police narratives and will ultimately feel

---

[7] Andy Myhill, *Community Engagement in Policing: Lessons from the Literature* (London: HMG Home Office, 2012), 17.

more comfortable to share their concerns and priorities with police. When police take community feedback seriously, this feedback shapes how police develop their priorities and take action, helping police be better at their jobs and increasing public confidence in police over time. Ideally, this creates a cycle of public confidence in which police use two-way engagement to communicate narratives and hear back from communities about concerns and priorities. Police then take the community feedback into account, modifying police priorities and practices in line with the community's views. This in turn generates greater public confidence in the police, making the community yet more receptive to the idea of engaging with police in the future.

Police can best maintain this cycle of public confidence when they develop a broad range of partnerships across communities using two-way engagement. Police often engage with prominent public figures such as local government officials or high-level religious leaders.[8] Because of the complexities of CVE work, police repeatedly seek out partners who lead public agencies and civil society organizations. These relationships are critical, but it is vital for police to reach beyond community leaders alone. In many cases, civil society leaders can assist police in accessing a segment of the local community, but these individuals also may overrepresent their influence and the extent to which they are seen as credible within their own communities.

Martin Innes, a criminologist based at Cardiff University, has written extensively about the importance of broad community engagement within the context of counterterrorism. He captures the importance of police connecting with diverse parts of their communities and highlights the

---

[8] "Think beyond old men in churches and mosques. Ensure that understanding of the religious sector reflects the relevance of actors beyond formal religious authorities and official institutions. Women, younger religious leaders, and traditionalist faith practices are key players in the religious landscape and often more influential than their formal and titled religious counterparts." See Peter Mandaville and Melissa Nozell, *Engaging Religion and Religious Actors in Countering Violent Extremism*, USIP Special Report 413 (Washington, DC: United States Institute of Peace, August 2017), https://www.usip.org/sites/default/files/SR413-Engaging-Religion-and-Religious-Actors-in-Countering-Violent-Extremism.pdf.

shortcomings of approaches that rely exclusively on relationships with senior community representatives:

> By identifying individual members of particular communities as leaders and/or opinion formers, police are seeking to establish contact with people who are most likely to be able to help them to accomplish their objectives. In so doing, however, it is of vital importance to be able to connect with the right people... It is difficult to know who really represents a community's views. Similarly, there must be a concern about whether community leaders are really in touch with those most at risk of alienation and radicalization... Police strategic engagements seek to instigate "strong ties" to key individuals located within particular communities. But . . . especially in situations where information is diffusely located, an extensive social network of weak ties has greater utility than a more restricted network of strong ties. Applied to issues of counterterrorism, where the key pieces of intelligence may well be diffusely located among different community members, it would seem that police strategic engagements need to be supplemented with a far more extensive network of community contacts.[9]

Innes clarifies the importance of developing a network of connections that includes diverse perspectives to capture the concerns and priorities of the broadest possible range of community members. Although in common parlance we use a single word for "community," communities are highly complex and made up of different, often divided, groups living together in a single place. Police have the challenging task of engaging the entire community and bringing their narratives to the many groups that make up the wider community. To do this, police should develop connections

---

[9] Martin Innes, "Policing Uncertainty: Countering Terror through Community Intelligence and Democratic Policing," *ANNALS of the American Academy of Political and Social Science* 605, no. 1 (May 2006): 13–14.

with as many of the different groups that make up the wider community as possible.

When police maintain partnerships across the wide community network, they can maximize their awareness of the community's concerns and priorities. Police centrality in the community network allows police to communicate narratives across different groups and in partnership with different messengers who hold credibility in their respective groups.

These findings are echoed in the author's research that highlights some of the challenges where police rely solely on select community representatives as partners in their CVE efforts. In cities where police partnered only with prominent community leaders, the impact of their CVE efforts was often more limited. By contrast, in cities where police invested in broad, two-way engagement, partnering with youth, women, police opponents, and other groups, police managed to gain the support of diverse constituents in communities that previously had weak relationships with local police. In some instances, these groups in the community became informal partners with police, enabling police to have a fuller picture of concerns and priorities held by the wider community. Police in turn modified their activities in line with community feedback.

In sum, police should engage with obvious stakeholders and community leaders but they need to go beyond these individuals to engage with police opponents, youth, women, and other groups that often represent different interests. Ultimately, police cannot afford to miss less prominent voices. When police go to the grassroots level, they often find new networks of individuals who can be powerful messengers and advance the work of CVE in critical ways. Police need to recognize that no single group can by itself advance CVE objectives across the whole community. Smaller groups in the community can support community policing in different ways. Police need to be present and engage in two-way community engagement with each of these groups, as highlighted in a hypothetical community network presented in figure 5.1.

Figure 5.1. The wheel of partnerships

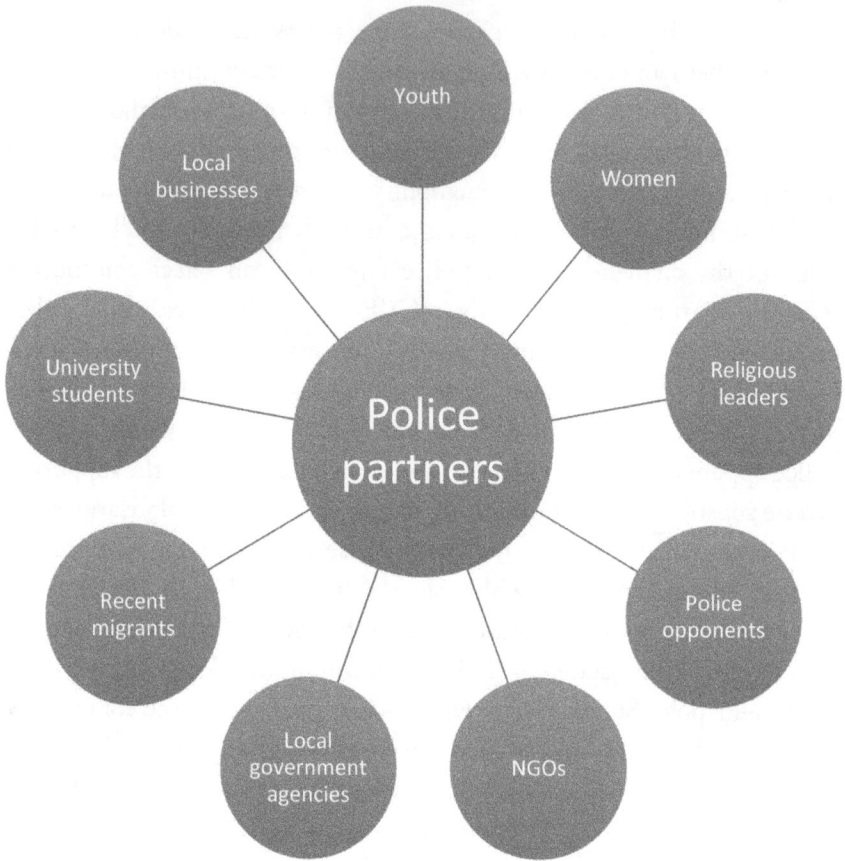

A police department's CVE efforts will benefit from direct connections with the smaller groups that make up the wider community network. For example, religious leaders are potential allies in countering violent extremism. They may communicate with police about visiting speakers who try to incite violence, and they may be aware of individuals who may become involved in terrorism. Religious leaders also frequently need assistance from police. Engagement with religious leaders can help inform police about instances where greater police protection is needed, perhaps around a particular holiday or event. However, these relationships need to be pursued carefully in order to avoid the appearance of co-opting religious leaders and institutions to become part of the police's security agendas. Police must ensure they develop authentically two-way relationships with religious leaders that prioritize leaders' concerns even when they do not pertain directly to CVE. Although religious leaders are important collaborators for police, they represent only one part of the community and they can be disconnected from other parts of local community networks. If police engage solely with religious leaders, police risk being unaware of violent extremism outside a religious context.

Police should also include young people in their CVE efforts.[10] Young people are often the targets of punitive police action and in many cases have lower levels of trust in the police.[11] Police need to dedicate energy to facilitating positive engagements with young people. One mechanism for engaging young people is through consultation, where police create a space to hear concerns directly from young people. Through such efforts, police can build direct relationships with youth that form the basis of future partnerships to address a range of community safety issues—beginning to shift traditionally negative one-directional interactions toward two-way cooperation.

Women are valuable partners in advancing community policing and CVE objectives specifically.[12] Police should include engagement with women as part of their wider strategy for community engagement. Women may have insights about crimes that target them, and they can inform police about security needs in their communities. Female family members

---

[10] Erin Saltman and Jas Kirt, "Guidance for International Youth Engagement in PVE and CVE,"
https://www.isdglobal.org/wp-content/uploads/2016/06/YouthCAN-UN-PVE-Survey.pdf.

[11] Alan Travis, "'Significant' Proportion of Children Distrust Police, Inquiry Finds," *Guardian*, October 28, 2014, https://www.theguardian.com/uk-news/2014/oct/28/significant-proportion-children-distrust-police-inquiry-all-party-parliamentary-report; and Jenny Jones, "Young People in This Country Don't Trust Our Police," *Independent*, January 10, 2013, https://www.independent.co.uk/voices/comment/young-people-in-this-country-dont-trust-our-police-8444833.html.

[12] Council on Foreign Relations, "Countering Violent Extremism by Engaging Women" (transcript of a symposium, held December 7, 2016), https://www.cfr.org/event/countering-violent-extremism-engaging-women.

are also potential allies in identifying and challenging violent extremism in their social networks.[13]

Police can enhance public confidence and advance CVE objectives when they develop relationships with diverse groups throughout the community. Together, these local partnerships can be a powerful resource for police in protecting public safety broadly and working to counter violent extremism. Through this engagement, police will hear back from communities about how to provide public protection better and improve the way they do their jobs.

Bringing Narratives to Groups in the Community

When developing engagement strategies, police should first think about how their community is interfacing with police and the unique features of the local community. Some groups—such as youth and women—exist in every city. However, there may be specific groups—such as recent migrant communities or smaller religious communities— that are unique to a particular city.

Having identified the various groups that make up the wider community, police should think critically about how each of these groups is currently being engaged by police. For example, in one city, police had strong relationships with local politicians and religious leaders from the city's largest, long-settled ethnic minority group. Police frequently held well-attended consultation events with local religious leaders and worked in close partnership with a community organization that brought together various civil society organizations—largely representing this one ethnic group.

Police leaders charged with delivering CVE programming realized,

---

[13] Edit Schlaffer and Ulrich Kropiunigg, "A New Security Architecture: Mothers Included!," in *A Man's World? Exploring the Roles of Women in Countering Terrorism and Violent Extremism*, ed. Naureen Chowdhury Fink, Sara Zeiger, and Rafia Bhulai (Abu Dhabi and Washington, DC: Hedayah and the Global Center on Cooperative Security, 2016); and Dina Temple-Raston, "The Female Quran Experts Fighting Radical Islam in Morocco," *Atlantic*, February 12, 2018, https://www.theatlantic.com/international/archive/2018/02/the-female-quran-experts-fighting-radical-islam-in-morocco/551996/.

however, that they needed to increase two-way engagement with several groups: women, recent migrant communities, university students, and opponents of the police. These groups had been little engaged by police. In particular, a recent migrant group was less integrated within existing civil society structures and was thus engaged at lower levels by police. Police recognized that all these groups were under-engaged and that the police should prioritize engagement with them. Police focused heavily on engaging recent migrants and police opponents. Police reached out to existing gatherings of women and youth from a recent migrant community to begin building relationships and provide reassurance using police narratives. They introduced themselves and sought to understand what the community needed. From these engagements, police began to improve relations with this group, who presented concerns about discrimination that they wanted police to address as well as other safety priorities. Police worked to respond to these concerns and maintain channels of open communication, opening up new partnerships that advanced community policing and CVE in the long term.

Police also made an effort to engage with individuals who opposed law enforcement activities and typically shied away from engaging with police. This involved investing energy in listening to and understanding the concerns of police opponents, as well as describing the intentions of the police to protect and support those at risk of being drawn into terrorism. In effect, police put forth a narrative about police providing protection to police opponents at various community events and forums as well as via social media for a wider audience. At some level, these activities produced a new level of understanding with some of the individuals who had avoided interfacing with police before, opening new areas of limited collaboration despite continued areas of disagreement.

Using these examples as a guide, police should be aware of the many groups that comprise their local community and identify those that are systematically under-engaged by police. Police can then think about how to organize two-way engagement with smaller groups.

Among the questions that can guide police in building a new approach to engagement are these three:

- What concerns might this group have that police could assist with?

- What is something this specific community might like from their police that could be better provided?
- How can we engage this group directly?

The answers to these questions can provide insight into how police can begin to reform their engagement strategies.

Through two-way engagement, police can ensure their narratives reach deeper into the local community. Moreover, police can create ties with a wider range of community partners, ensuring that they better understand risks and concerns in the community. By pursuing responsive policing, police can begin to build greater public confidence and enrich efforts to counter violent extremism over time.

The rest of this chapter highlights how police have engaged smaller groups within their communities. These examples are intended to guide police in diverse contexts in their own efforts to widen their community partnerships as part of their CVE efforts.

Engaging with Women

As already discussed, women can be valuable allies for community policing in general and for CVE efforts specifically. Women may have insights about areas where additional police protection is needed to mitigate crime or they may be aware of violent extremism in their social circles.

In one city, police sought to enhance their CVE programing. They had been using strategic narratives and two-way engagement with city councilors and leaders of community organizations, many of whom were elder males. Police officers recognized that they needed to build relationships and create confidence across the wider community network, and they focused specifically on addressing gaps in public confidence among women. To forge relationships, police used openings created by regular community policing activities. When police learned that a small community of minority women were being targeted for gold jewelry theft, police quickly arrested the offending individuals. But police also wanted to communicate narratives to women in the community. To do this, police engaged with the victims of these thefts, explaining their intentions to provide a service to the community and to respond to concerns these women had about public safety in the future. The combination of practically providing protection with the strategic use of narratives created an opening to begin to establish partnerships and build confidence, where they had been absent previously.

In another city where several individuals had left as foreign fighters to join the Islamic State, local police officers worked to improve engagement with women using a proactive approach. Several female police officers led an International Women's Day event in which they convened representatives of local services agencies, female business leaders, and members of civil society to discuss violent extremism, as well as other issues of concern, such as women's leadership and domestic abuse. Local police officers discussed their CVE efforts, including efforts to stop at-risk individuals from being drawn into terrorism, as well as other safeguarding initiatives relevant to women. This event provided an opportunity for local police to introduce themselves to women in the community, to present the police's narratives, and to invite the community to partner with the police in their CVE work.

The International Women's Day event was particularly valuable because it created a safe space for local police and women in the community to discuss violent extremism and engage with police narratives. Out of this conference, police fostered two-way engagement and created long-term partnerships with women in the community who had previously had little interaction with local police. This was a marked improvement over earlier approaches in which police engaged largely with male community representatives who were expected to speak on behalf of women in the community.

Engaging with Youth

There is sometimes an unfortunate assumption that young people have adversarial relationships with police and cannot make positive contributions to community policing. In reality, young people can serve as valuable allies, helping police better understand their communities and build new partnerships with a wider range of community members.

In one city, police wanted to increase their engagement with young people to challenge violent extremism. Police collaborated with youth to make a video about terrorism and educate school children about what to do when they had concerns about individuals becoming involved in terrorism. Instead of police visiting a local school and lecturing about counterterrorism and the obligations of youth to support CVE, police and youth worked together to produce a video and establish protocols about how youth could work with police to address violent extremism in the future.

The process of making the video increased face-to-face time between officers and youth and provided informal opportunities for police to establish relationships with young people. Police were also able to communicate police narratives outside of a criminal context, laying the foundation for future partnerships.

In several other cities, police used more structured approaches to make inroads with young people. One common strategy was organizing youth consultation boards, which involved selecting a small and diverse group of youth representatives who meet with police on a regular basis. Youth on the consultation boards were able to speak about their concerns and priorities and have them heard by police and reflected in police activity. In another city, police organized a "Police Week" at a local university; the police team charged with delivering CVE programs set up a table with information about police and safety tips. Students could them approach them, ask questions and get information, and begin building relationships. A demonstrated willingness to listen to young people can create valuable openings for police to present narratives and pursue responsive policing that builds public confidence over time.

Engaging with Religious Communities

Religious leaders should also be a priority for two-way engagement. Police should hold events to reiterate their commitment to protect religious spaces and to inform communities about how to speak with police if they have public safety concerns. In one city where police had few existing connections to local religious leadership, police asked to attend the meeting of a local religious association which provided an opportunity for police to learn about community needs and concerns. Similar to the example of police visiting a university to answer questions, being publicly visible in religious spaces, providing assurance, and communicating a narrative of protection can be an effective way of developing partnerships with the community. These kinds of engagements begin to create openings for partnerships in the future, making it possible for local religious leaders to bring forward concerns or request additional protection from police on particular occasions. When police respond effectively to concerns expressed by the community, public confidence in the police can begin to grow.

It is important to stress that police must be highly responsive to the concerns religious communities have about their safety, such as hate crimes that actively target them. Especially in the context of CVE, police can build stronger relationships with religious communities when police actively prioritize the safety of minority communities, addressing hate crime and discrimination with the same determination as they attempt to counter violent extremism. In practice, this means that police should record and respond to instances of hate crime with the same thoroughness that they dedicate to countering violent extremism. Police should actively protect religious spaces from violence and be prepared to challenge all forms of violent extremism. If police fail to vigorously challenge all forms of extremism, they risk targeting and alienating smaller groups in the community and setting back public confidence in the police. When police prioritize community concerns—even when the concerns do not directly pertain to CVE—police narratives become tangible for communities, thereby mitigating concerns that police claim to be providing protection but in fact are targeting religious groups for counterterrorism intelligence.

Engaging with Public Agencies

Finally, public service workers in local government agencies can serve as valuable allies in CVE. Although police are often the first to be trained about CVE, there are many aspects of CVE that police should delegate to public agencies. Police can do their jobs more effectively when they build sustained and mutually beneficial relationships with representatives of public agencies, including social workers and educators.

Police have used a number of approaches to build connections with public agencies around CVE. One common approach is to establish a counter extremism task force or advisory body that combines civil society representatives, police, and representatives of local agencies, such as health workers, schoolteachers, and elected local government leaders. Together, various agencies work together to draft plans about CVE programming and design strategies that respond to local concerns. This collaboration makes police aware of the expertise of various public agencies, in turn strengthening ties and trust between these agencies and police.

Another effective way for police to build partnerships with local agencies is to lead a "train the trainer" session with various local agencies. Through these sessions, police can educate local service providers about CVE; the service providers can then share the information within their own organizations. Police can use these training opportunities to clarify what aspects of CVE they focus on and how local agencies can communicate with police. These trainings are a good way for police to answer questions so that they and a range of local agencies share the same understanding about CVE and work collaboratively to address risks in the community.

Summary

Police can advance the work of CVE when they use narratives and two-way engagement with the many groups that make up the wider communities. Although police do not need to constantly consult with every group in their community, they should invest in building long-term partnerships across their community networks. This chapter presents examples to guide police in establishing partnerships with various groups in the community, including youth, religious leaders, women, and local service providers. Police can reach out to these and other groups in the community with narratives, partnering with community members to address community safety and violent extremism. These activities can help to improve public confidence in the police over time.

CHAPTER 6
BRINGING NARRATIVES TO SOCIAL MEDIA

TALENE BILAZARIAN

Executive Summary

- Social media can enhance engagement with communities and help build public confidence in the police.
- Police should use narratives on social media to amplify their offline CVE and community policing efforts.
- Police organizations all over the world already use social media, providing important sources of good practice.

Introduction

The importance of two-way engagement between police and communities, as well as the need for police to develop a diverse network of ties across community networks, has been discussed in previous chapters. This chapter addresses a related topic: how police can use social media to support a cycle of two-way engagement and confidence building. The chapter begins by showing how police can use social media to reach out to their communities and listen to community concerns and priorities to advance community policing. It then discusses how police can use social media to present themselves to local communities, bringing their narratives forward to interact with other ideas communities may have about them. The chapter concludes by providing strategies to maximize the effectiveness of police presence on social media. It presents examples of the kind of content police should post online and offers tips on how to manage social media accounts and how to maintain a safe online presence.

Social media can be a tool to mirror and amplify what police are already doing in the community. Although this chapter discusses social media good practices for police, the aim is to put social media usage in context as one tool in the wider police toolkit. Police can advance and integrate key principles—particularly the use of narratives to build public confidence—online. Social media is a space for police to present their narratives, especially to those community members who may be unable or reluctant to engage with police offline.

Why Does Social Media Matter?

Social media has fundamentally changed the way individuals connect— in 2018, more than 2.5 billion people used social media.[1] Because social media is a means of facilitating connection and sharing information, police should establish a social media presence to ensure that they are part of a wider conversation, providing information to and hearing back from communities digitally.

A Community Forum

Social media is an especially important forum for police because it is a place where the reputations of police are repeatedly debated. Police must bring their narratives to the table because social media is a space where the public can engage in an ongoing conversation about whether or not the police are legitimately providing protection. Online, communities may portray

---

[1] Statistics Portal, "Number of Social Media Users Worldwide from 2010 to 2021," https://www.statista.com/statistics/278414/number-of-worldwide-social-network-users/.

police as perpetrators of abuse and wrongful arrests who target youth and minorities. In many cases, these grievances are legitimate and should be addressed offline with clear investment in police reform. However, negative views of police can clash sharply with how police would like the public to understand them and their goals. In light of such a discrepancy, police must represent themselves honestly online—communicating narratives about their good work in the community and being realistic about areas for improvement—because no one else will do this for them.

A Tool for Community Policing

Social media has changed the way that police services do their jobs.[2] It is used as a tool to conduct investigations and alert the public about security. A survey of nearly six hundred North American police forces conducted in 2016 by the International Association of Chiefs of Police and the Urban Institute found that 96 percent of police services were using some kind of social media.[3] A similar survey in 2015 showed that more than 80 percent of surveyed agencies said that social media improved police-community relations.[4] These results indicate that social media is an important tool in broader community policing efforts.

* * *

The following sections lay out broad strategies and specific guidance to help police use social media effectively to communicate narratives about

---

[2] IACP Center for Social Media, "2012 IACP Social Media Survey," http://www. iacpsocialmedia.org/wp-content/uploads/2017/01/2012SurveyResults.pdf.

[3] KiDeuk Kim, Ashlin Oglesby-Neal, and Edward Mohr, *2016 Law Enforcement Use of Social Media Survey: A Joint Publication by the International Association of Chiefs of Police and the Urban Institute* (Urban Institute and International Association of Chiefs of Police, 2016), https://www.urban.org/sites/default/files/publication/88661/2016-law-enforcement-use-of-social-media-survey_5.pdf.

[4] IACP Center for Social Media, "International Association of Chiefs of Police 2015 Social Media Survey," http://www.iacpsocialmedia.org/wp-content/uploads/2017/01/FULL-2015-Social-Media-Survey-Results.compressed.pdf.

themselves while maintaining security and professionalism over the long term.

There are many examples of criticism about police and police abuses on social media. A brief search on Twitter in summer 2017 revealed community members around the world describing police brutality, ranging from social organizing in opposition to police activity across the United States to discussions of police discrimination and brutality in Latin America and the Middle East. Police can best address such concerns through effective community policing, using two-way engagement and responsive policing that works with, not against, community members.

Police can also amplify good policing on the ground by representing themselves well online. As the examples in this chapter illustrate, police can publicize their efforts to engage local communities and can share security tips or information. Police can also use social media to humanize themselves by employing humor and heartwarming stories, as well as by outlining areas for improvement.

Proactive and Reactive Engagement

Police use social media to deliver a variety of content to their communities, but the use of social media generally falls into two categories: proactive engagement and reactive engagement.

Proactive Engagement

With proactive engagement, police create or control a situation, reaching out in the two-way interaction to communicate priorities or actions back to the community, typically outside of an emergency context. One form of proactive engagement is publicizing ordinary policing activities in the community, such as making an arrest or organizing a neighborhood watch scheme. Police often publicize opportunities for the community to interact with police or use social media to communicate that they are organizing a consultation opportunity, inviting the community into a two-way interaction. The following anonymized examples illustrate how police forces have used social media for community engagement; these are examples, not endorsements.

- In one South Asian capital city, police publicized consultation and two-way engagement. Police posted pictures of a women's consultation event on Facebook and commented about their commitment to work with the women gathered to create a safer city
- Other police services have used Twitter to invite the public to consult with them, using it as a platform to notify a wider group of people of upcoming consultation events
- Still others have invited the public to engage with them on a foot patrol, posting photos of officers at work on Twitter with encouragement to engage and interact with officers.

Police frequently use social media to inform communities about successful police activity. Take, for example, this tweet by the Cambridge Police Department (in Massachusetts): "Crowds have been dispersed and cleared from Galleria area. 6 juveniles were arrested 4 disorderly conduct, disturbing the peace & trespassing."

Another example of proactive engagement is when police reach out to provide transparency about the challenges associated with their job and highlight potential areas for improvement. These types of interactions online help humanize police.

Another beneficial form of proactive engagement online is program postings that alert the public of nonemergency services provided by the police. For example, one police force notified the public about a service to protect bicycles and evaluate the security of homes and work places. Various police forces have used social media to recruit individuals to join their departments, presenting an open call that communicates who the police are, what they do, and how others can be part of their organization.

Police also use social media proactively to share security tips or information. Some police services have used various social media platforms to provide information on preventing car break-ins or thefts.

The police in Cambridge, Massachusetts, use social media to share news about police dogs, providing a humanizing angle on policing: "It's #NationalDogDay. In celebration, we're posting some photos of our hard-working bomb dogs, who respond to suspicious package calls, bomb threats or other similar incidents to keep the Cambridge community safe."

Humor can also be integrated effectively into the wider social media presence of police, which can help to diversify content and drive broader engagement with police on social media. Examples includes using sarcasm to highlight the importance of safe driving and self-deprecating depictions of police on donut runs. Using social media proactively can help humanize police, portraying them as public servants who interact with the community in the face of real challenges, at times with a sense of humor. As the above examples show, proactive engagement publicizes positive police work, opportunities for interactions with police, and services police provide to the community. It can also create opportunities to demonstrate the humanity of the police. More important, proactive engagement on social media can allow police to demonstrate their intention to provide better public protection and their awareness of current shortcomings.

Reactive Engagement

With proactive engagement, police are the initiators on social media. They reach out with information they want the community to have about how to keep themselves safe or how to understand police. In reactive engagement, police respond to crimes, concerns, and other community dynamics. As reactors, police aim to provide information or context to benefit the community. The most common examples of reactive engagement on social media are when police provide reassurance in response to an emergency or ask for information from the community about crimes.

The NYPD, noting the importance of using social media reactively to provide information, cites the example of when a train was derailed and caused extensive injuries. The department provided information on the situation via social media to allay fears, helping government agencies and other followers to stay informed.[5]

In another example, when there was disruptive police activity in a

---

[5] William Bratton, "Orientation: NYPD Social Media Rollout" (New York Police Department, June 23, 2014), https://www.scribd.com/document/249158781/NYPD-Twitter-Strategy.

neighborhood where police were confronting local gang members, the NYPD provided information on the situation via social media and directed residents to remain calm, providing some reassurance during a period of heightened insecurity.[6]

Police also may use social media to update the community about road interruptions, establishing themselves as a credible source for live updates that can be readily shared by public agencies and by journalists online.

Social media is commonly used to elicit information about missing people and suspected individuals, or to get tips from the public that can help a wide range of crimes. Because of the ease of engagement on social media platforms, this might help to engage a wider swath of the community and elicit tips from potential bystanders and witnesses.

To sum up, police should use a mix of reactive and proactive engagement. Constant proactive engagement that publicizes consultation opportunities in the style of "come and speak with us" and trust-building messages in the style of "we're doing great work" can begin to feel detached from challenges and uncertainties that communities face, jeopardizing the communication of narratives. To maximize community reception on social media, police must maintain a two-way conversation in which they recognize shortcomings, converse with the community online, and respond to real issues offline.

Strategies for Integrating Social Media, Community Engagement, and Narratives

Police departments can employ several strategies for integrating social media, community engagement, and narratives.

---

[6] Ibid.

Use Social Media for Community Consultation

Social media can act as a consultation forum in itself. Seattle police used social media to create a virtual town hall.[7] Community members were asked to send comments and questions to police in advance; the police chief then responded to the comments and answered the questions on social media. This model can be used in a variety of contexts and allows police to respond to and establish a connection with a wide range of community members, including those who might be reluctant or unable to attend an in-person consultation. It is important, however, to ensure that police protect the privacy of community members and that community members' identities are not revealed or attributed to specific comments or questions without consent.

Conduct Tweet-Alongs

Police have used "tweet-alongs," or virtual ride-alongs, where a neighborhood police team provides community members with virtual access to one of its neighborhood patrols, tweeting photos and videos throughout the tour. Tweet-alongs give communities a visual insight into the routine of community policing and a view of the neighborhood from the perspective of the police.[8]

Support Community Events

Police can use their social media presence to support community events that relate to CVE or other community welfare priorities. For instance, police can promote blood drives or other volunteering efforts or events

[7] Kaveh Waddell, "The Police Office 'Nextdoor,'" *Atlantic*, May 4, 2016, https://www.theatlantic.com/technology/archive/2016/05/nextdoor-social-network-police-seattle/481164/.

[8] Bratton, "Orientation"; and Community Oriented Policing Service, "Awareness Briefing: Online Radicalization to Violent Extremism," https://ric-zai-inc.com/Publications/cops-w0739-pub.pdf; http://www.theiacp.org/portals/0/pdfs/radicalizationtoviolentextremismawarenessbrief.pdf.

that challenge violent extremism outside a traditional policing perspective. Such efforts demonstrate that police are engaged in the community's development and that they are actively promoting the community's interests.

Social Media Practices

To take advantage of the benefits that social media offers in terms of communicating police narratives, police organizations should employ certain practices.

Be Honest and Transparent

Police should use social media to contextualize and explain heavy-handed police action that jeopardizes their narratives. On many social media accounts, police appear to post only about their successes. They describe meeting with prestigious figures or list the honors they have received. Although this approach is understandable, the unvarying projection of a positive image often does not align with how communities actually view their police. When there is a wide gap between how communities experience their police locally and how police present themselves online, police using social media becomes merely broadcasting propaganda rather than providing a valuable service. This rapidly delegitimizes the police presence on social media, turning it into a publicity exercise.

Honesty helps police establish credibility because it shows that police are aware of their own shortcomings and are realistic about areas in need of improvement. Police have discretion about how and when they share their shortcomings and areas for improvement. Certainly, police need to exercise sensitivity and ensure that the content they post does not compromise individuals nor broader police work, especially around ongoing investigations or in regard to the identities of individual community members.

However, it is important to stress that police should think about how to maximize transparency online, especially in areas where police recognize that they need to do better. Police are often reluctant to reveal mistakes and shortcomings online, but made tactfully and appropriately, such admissions can provide context to police action. Moreover, they help police gain control over their narratives. When police share information about smaller mistakes, this honesty demonstrates the police commitment to provide better public protection in the future, even when they have fallen short in action.

For instance, a police officer apologized for startling a motorist by accidentally activating their emergency lights. In another instance, police in England misidentified several young people that they thought were involved in criminal activity. When they realized that they had made a mistake, they addressed the mistake on social media. They also invited these young people to join a youth consulting effort to rebuild relationships with individuals who had been mistreated by police. These examples demonstrate how online police activity can also connect to offline community engagement.

Carefully Manage the Online Presence

Police at all levels should think carefully about how they manage their presence on social media because it represents the work of the wider force. Because social media is designed to deepen connections across a community, content from officers at all levels should be represented on social media. At the same time, police on social media must maintain a high level of professionalism, constantly mindful that inappropriate postings by one or more officers could jeopardize the legitimacy of the police force as a whole.

Police departments might give the officer leading each neighborhood team a neighborhood account and allow that person to post approved content, once policies and procedures on various platforms and tools have been established. In other departments, police forces have one central account; posts are approved by social media coordinators for the whole department. The division of authority is ultimately an area of flexibility and negotiation, where the goal is to strike a balance between presenting local perspectives while making sure that social media content represents the wider force.

It is important for leadership at the highest levels to use social media and to lead by example, particularly in regard to messaging about shortcomings. When senior police officers use social media, they can establish norms and best practices around being transparent and use proactive and reactive online engagement that can serve as examples to lower-level officers.

Share Appropriate Content

Social media is a tool like any other, and how police use it determines whether it is useful or damaging to broader police work. Figure 6.1, which was developed by the Cambridge, Massachusetts, Police Department, provides a guide for thinking about how police should share content on social media. It highlights that police can drive more engagement on social media when they share a range of different content: trust-building posts that create solidarity between police and communities; reminders and information; and time-sensitive alerts and requests for information.

Figure 6.1. Content for police on social media

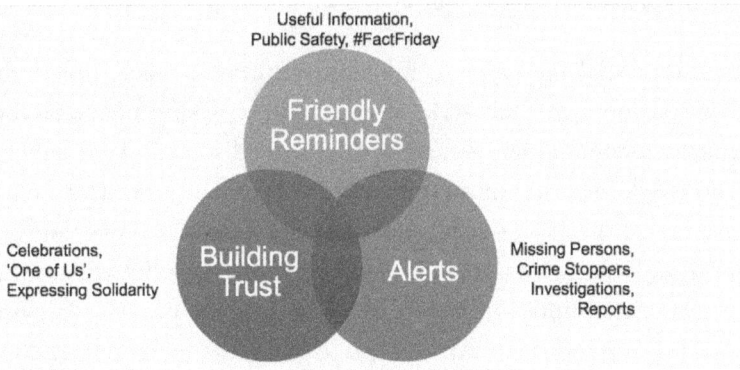

Source: Provided by the City of Cambridge, Massachusetts, and the Cambridge, Massachusetts, Police Department.

The NYPD's manual on social media delves into detail about content, outlining beneficial content and topics to avoid. [9] The department offers numerous examples of suitable online content, ranging from advisories and alerts to crime prevention tips, examples of exceptional police work, holiday notices, information about other agencies, and expressions of appreciation toward community groups.

The NYPD also lists content that should be avoided, including the following:[10]

- Crime scene information and photos
- Ongoing police investigations
- Police jargon
- Compromising photos or information about public individuals or groups
- Information that is confidential in nature
- Personal contact information

Use an Appropriate Style and Strategy

Because social media is an inherently informal space, police should be conversational in their style of engagement. Using police jargon or too much self-congratulation makes police seem distant and not public servants who are close to the community and aware of local priorities. Police should ensure that their social media posts are clear, conversational, and searchable for those looking for the kinds of information the police are posting online.

Another important aspect of a social media presence is gaining and maintaining followers. An easy place to start is by following community organizations and media organizations. Unlike offline, where they are quickly identifiable because of their uniforms, police are easier to miss online. However, they become more noticeable when they post content and interact with other groups and individuals online. This then creates

[9] William Bratton, "Orientation: NYPD Social Media Rollout" (New York Police Department, June 23, 2014), https://www.scribd.com/document/249158781/NYPD-Twitter-Strategy
[10] Ibid.

the opportunity for other social media users to respond by following police and interacting with them online.

Social media is of little importance if no one is paying attention to it, so police should consider carefully how to maintain followers to ensure their social media strategy is impactful. Staging an online town hall might generate attention in a short period of time. Sharing and promoting local programs, events, and initiatives that are doing positive things in the community can help police to build links with a range of local agencies and civil society groups that may fall outside their immediate police networks. This kind of interaction also signals that police are involved in the wider well-being of the community, rather than simply using social media as a public relations tool. New users who encounter police on social media through other users may choose to follow the police. As part of this broader strategy, police should aim to reply and respond promptly to people who engage with them online. If a community member makes an effort to interact online with a request or question, responding shows that police care about their community and that police are using social media to assist local communities.

Social media has some linguistic anomalies that vary between platforms. For instance, the symbol @ and the hashtag sign # are important for communicating on Twitter.[11] When police want their messages to be seen by particular accounts on Twitter—for instance, on a civil society organization's newsfeed—they should use the @ symbol, including @ theindividual'sname in the post, which is known as a Twitter "handle." For instance, the United States Institute of Peace's Twitter handle is @USIP. If police want to speak to a user privately, they can use the direct message function of the social media platform.

Police should use hashtags strategically to ensure their messages reach their target audiences and are easily searchable. For instance, use the hashtag of the precinct, the kind of crime, or the event they are posting about online. One particular hashtag may be used widely for a local event such as a parade, a blood drive, or a community festival; police should follow the conventions of the audience they are trying to reach. If police

---

[11] *Wired* Staff, "How to Use Twitter: Critical Tips for New Users," *Wired,* May 2016, https://www.wired.com/2016/05/twitter-onboarding-tips-for-new-users/.

tweet about a subject to express solidarity or provide information, they should make sure to use the appropriate hashtag.

While this chapter has focused on examples of police on Twitter and Facebook, police organizations use a wide range of social media, including Instagram. Instagram is a highly visual medium, and police have used it to share pictures and videos of police engaging with members of the community, creating a visual narrative of police providing protection to members of the public. For instance, Officer Tommy Norman from Little Rock, Arkansas, received significant press attention and acquired a large social media following for his adept use of Instagram to capture community policing activities.[12] His Instagram account features pictures and videos of engagement with a wide range of community members, particularly young people. While the particularities of specific social media tools vary, the broad strategic principles for police are largely similar. One way that police can improve their use of different social media platforms is by observing other police services' accounts. These can provide valuable examples of how to use social media to advance policing objectives in a variety of circumstances and on a range of platforms, updated in real time.

Continually Monitor and Refine the Social Media Presence

As police use social media as part of their broader engagement strategy, they should continually be monitoring themselves and their content. What kind of posts are liked and reposted? Which have a small or largely negative reception? Self-monitoring can provide informal guidance on how the community wants to interact with police online. Based on such an ongoing assessment, police should continually refine the online content they produce.

Police should strive for content that their communities find informative,

---

[12] Joe McCarthy, "Can All Police Officers Be Like This Cop?" *Global Citizen*, July 13, 2016. https://www.globalcitizen.org/en/content/officer-tommy-norman-community-policing-the-game/; and Katie Rogers, "The New Officer Friendly, Armed With Instagram, Tweets and Emojis," *New York Times*, July 13, 2016, https://www.nytimes.com/2016/07/13/us/the-new-officer-friendly-armed-with-instagram-tweets-and-emojis.html.

useful, and shareable. Beyond analyzing individual posts and their public reception, police should notice the overall number of followers, information that is typically found on the main profile page of a social media website. If a particular social media effort, such as a tweet-along, wins many new followers, assess this trend internally and attempt to integrate similar efforts more regularly into the online presence.

Police should spend the time to polish their profile—both the photograph and the biography that appear to other users on social media. The social media profile is a chance to visually depict and quickly summarize a narrative about the police, encapsulating the online face of police to the community. Police departments should carefully select a photograph that shows police officers serving the community and add a biography that briefly communicates police narratives.

Maintain Security

Online security is vitally important. Police must ensure that their presence online is protected from those who seek to damage that presence. At the most basic level, individuals should use official computers and devices whenever they use social media in a police capacity. Personal phones and computers are likely to be less secure than departmental devices. Individuals should select hard-to-guess passwords that should not be shared.

When signing on to social media, the individual managing the account should always use two-factor authentication.[13] Two-factor authentication asks that a user to sign in with a password as well as with a code that is sent to the user. Officers should install software updates as needed and keep antivirus software up to date. These basic measures will help limit the likelihood that a departmental computer or device will be infected by a virus or accessed by hackers.

Some social media platforms require police organizations to verify their accounts. For instance, on Twitter the user verifies his or her identity with Twitter and receives a blue checkmark in the profile indicating that the account is verified. It is vital that police accounts go through this

---

[13] *SecurEnvoy.* "What Is 2FA?" www.securenvoy.com/two-factor-authentication/what-is-2fa.shtm.

verification process; it communicates professionalism and ensures that journalists, public servants, and members of the community will not be confused about the identity of the account. It also decreases the likelihood that copycat accounts will jeopardize police narratives.[14]

Summary

Police should remember a few basic tips about their online presence. First, police should come across as relatable and human online. Second, people engage with police on social media to get information that helps them go about their daily life or to have an experience of connecting with police. Third, it is vital that police stay honest on social media—admitting shortcomings can increase the perception of trustworthiness. It shows self-awareness, and allows people to take police messages—the good and the bad—seriously. Police should be wary of holding back and being seen as dishonest or out of touch. Finally, police should ensure that they use social media as a tool to inform the community and to learn from it, using a combination of reactive and proactive engagement.

It is important to place the ideas presented in this chapter in the context of two-way engagement. Social media is a mirror of the offline work that police do. If police fail to engage and respond to community concerns offline, their presence on social media will have less impact when sharing narratives and trying to build long-term public confidence in the police. Police need to engage with and hear back from the community about concerns and priorities off-line in order for their narratives to resonate with communities online.

The long-term success of a social media campaign depends on how police translate actions offline and what they do with the information they encounter on social media. By prioritizing narratives, two-way community engagement, and responsive policing, police can make inroads toward building public confidence in police.

---

[14] *Wikihow*, "How to Get a Verified Account on Twitter," www.wikihow.com/Get-a-Verified-Account-on-Twitter.

CHAPTER 7

ORIENTING THE ORGANIZATIONAL CULTURE TO ENHANCE PUBLIC CONFIDENCE: A CHANGE MANAGEMENT MODEL

DAN WADDINGTON

Executive Summary

- Police services can use the information gleaned from an organizational assessment to reorient the organization.
- Organizational change is challenging, but it can be undertaken successfully if it is approached with a sound methodology, including a recognition of need, organizational buy-in, planning, training, and implementation.
- The SWOT analysis highlighted in Chapter 3 provides a process to address the first step in organizational change: recognition of need.
- Organizational buy-in must come from all levels of the organization, including executives, managers, supervisors, and line personnel.
- The police must establish strategies and identify strategic goals. SMART is a methodology for planning and achieving goals in

101

which goals are specific, measurable, achievable, relevant, and timely.
- Training is essential in the organizational change process.

Introduction

To create a positive narrative and enhance public confidence, a police organization must assess internal strengths and weaknesses and external threats and opportunities. Although self-understanding is key to this process, it is only the first step in a change management model. The next step is to develop an action plan.

Developing an action plan is analogous to orienteering. Orienteering is a competitive international sport that combines racing with navigation. It is a race in which participants use a specially created, highly detailed map to select routes and navigate through diverse, difficult, and often unfamiliar terrain. Police services are in a race against extremists to win the hearts and minds of their community members. But, as with a true orienteering effort, winning is not necessarily about how fast you run, but about how successfully you map out your course to get through the obstacles and challenges.

As discussed in chapter 3, a SWOT analysis helps a police service get the lay of the land. It provides an overview to help the organization understand where it is in CVE efforts and a view of the terrain and obstacles as the organization tries to shift language about the police with the goal of collaborating with the community to establish trust and confidence in the police service.

If the police organization lacks public trust and confidence, it must invalidate or undermine negative narratives. The only way to do this in a sustainable manner is by implementing organizational change. Although a major organizational change project can be highly rewarding to both the police service and the community it serves, it can be an extremely difficult undertaking. Change does not typically go over well in police organizations. Culturally, the majority of managers and executives do not tolerate failure. However, change is necessary in all organizations at some point, and police leaders must help their officers accept and prosper during change. Ultimately, leaders must realize that change is hard for everyone and many people will require guidance and encouragement throughout the process.

The organizational change process includes the following steps:

1. Recognize the need for change
2. Obtain organizational buy-in
3. Plan a SMART process
4. Conduct training
5. Draft and Implement a change plan

Recognize the Need for Change

The SWOT process helps an organization recognize the need for change. It summarizes internal strengths and weaknesses and external threats and opportunities. The information derived from this analysis can be used to scope out needs, communicate reasons for change, and provide input on the next step in the change management model.

Obtain Organizational Buy-In

It is important for managers to clearly communicate why change is necessary. Often, organizations fail to tell those who are impacted by a change why it is happening. For example, if a policy agency is trying to overcome negative narratives promoted by extremists, the administration can introduce new policies and procedures to eliminate brutality from police practices. However, if the reasons for the new policies are not communicated, the people impacted by them will make up their own reasons. They might see the new tactics as management bowing to the pressures of the extremists as opposed to voluntary efforts by the police to develop a positive, cooperative relationship with the communities the police are supposed to serve. When management rationale and line officers' assumptions do not align, the discrepancy can cause conflict and resentment and impede acceptance and application of new policies and procedures.

Change objectives must be communicated to the organization as a whole in order for all to embrace the change. Audiences include:

- Executives
- Managers
- Supervisors
- Line personnel

Resistance to change may come from police officials, especially those with long tenures. Because giving orders is the norm, many police officials fail to develop their managerial toolkit to include techniques for influencing, inspiring, or engaging officers. Although the police culture supports a structure in which orders and directives are carried out and cascaded to the frontline, that should not be read as support for or commitment to a change, even when imposed by officials. Purposeful employee engagement is required to fuel and sustain a change process.

Plan a SMART Process

To increase its chances of successfully implementing a major change effort, a police service needs a comprehensive and flexible implementation plan that is supported by its members.

David Bayley, a leading scholar on policing issues, states that a strategic plan must exist for organizational change to occur successfully.[11] Bayley explains that it may be necessary for specific pieces of the reform process to be in place before others are undertaken. For example, some fundamental systemic problems may have to exist before the organization is prepared to change the narrative in any meaningful way. The systematic self-assessment provided by a SWOT analysis offers a methodology to understand which issues to focus on. A SWOT analysis can help establish whether the preconditions exist (or need to be created) that will allow the organization to attempt to implement dependent objectives and programs.

To move from an assessment of where the organization is to a plan

---

[1] D. H. Bayley, *Changing the Guard: Developing Democratic Police Abroad* (New York: Oxford University Press, 2006).

for where it wants to be, a police service must articulate strategies and identify strategic goals. SMART is a tool used by organizations to plan and achieve goals. Although there are several interpretations of the acronym's meaning, a common one is "Specific, Measurable, Achievable, Relevant, and Timely." SMART can extend the capabilities of those working to achieve these goals while being rewarding for the organization and its members.[22]

Specific

An organization should make its goals as specific as possible so as not to cover too broad an area or require the completion of a large number of steps or the satisfaction of a vast array of objectives. Being specific also holds the organization more accountable to the goals. Specific goals specify what actions will be taken and by whom. Specific goals also help an agency determine if it has accomplished its objectives. A specific goal has a much greater chance of being accomplished than a general goal.

When drafting specific goals, a police organization should ask the five "W" questions:

- What do we want to accomplish?
- Why is this goal important?
- Who is involved?
- Where is it undertaken?
- Which resources or limits are involved?

Measurable

Organizations should break each goal down into measurable elements. Concrete criteria should be established for measuring progress toward the attainment of each goal. When an agency measures progress, it is more likely to stay on track, reach target dates, and experience the feeling of achievement that inspires staff to continue to make the efforts required

---

[2] R. Garner, "'SWOT' Tactics: Basics for Strategic Planning," *FBI Law Enforcement Bulletin* 74, no. 11 (2005): 17–19.

to reach the goal. The measure may be quantitative or qualitative, but it must allow judgments to be made against a standard of performance and a standard of expectation. Measurable goals can significantly help an organization define and refine exactly what it wants to achieve. Defining the physical manifestations of a goal or objective makes it clearer and easier to reach.

To determine if a goal is measurable, an organization should ask these questions:

- How much do we want?
- How many do we want?
- How will we know when our goal is accomplished?

Achievable

Those charged with pursuing goals must find them achievable and realistic in scope. Goals that have no reasonable chance of success do not help the organization or the individuals who must work toward the goal's completion. Some people, believing that they are providing challenging direction to an organization, may set goals so lofty or demanding that no one possibly can satisfy them, thereby dooming they the organization to fail—exactly the opposite of the intended effect.

To determine if a goal is achievable, an organization should ask these questions:

- How can we accomplish this goal?
- How realistic is the goal based on other constraints?

Relevant

Organizations must ensure that the goal matters and that it aligns with other relevant goals. They should avoid simplistic, easy, or meaningless goals. Goals should challenge the organization within its limits and extend the capabilities of those working to achieve them. Careful consideration in goal creation can lead to renewed enthusiasm for the agency and its mission.

To determine if a goal is relevant, an organization should ask these questions:

- Does this seem worthwhile?
- Is this the right time?
- Does this match our other efforts and needs?
- Is it applicable in the current environment?

Timely

Goals that are timely identify a specific issue that a department can accomplish in an appropriate time frame.

Every goal needs a target date—a deadline to focus on and something to work toward. This part of the SMART criteria helps prevent everyday tasks from taking priority over longer-term goals.

To determine if a goal is time bound, an organization should ask these questions:

- When?
- What can we do six months from now?
- What can we do six weeks from now?
- What can we do now?

Applying SMART: Addressing Police Brutality

The SWOT analysis generates ideas for specific goals and objectives for the strategic plan. Table 7.1 is based on the sample SWOT matrix discussed in chapter 3 (see figure 3.2).

Table 7.1: Sample SWOT matrix for addressing police brutality[3]

HELPFUL (INTERNAL) to establishing encouraging narratives	HURTFUL (INTERNAL) to establishing encouraging narratives
STRENGTHS	WEAKNESSES
S1. Police officials and commissioned officers have been receptive and responsive to new policing philosophies.	W1. The police organization is very large and unwieldy.
S2. Community engagement principles have been positively received by police officers and executives.	W2. History of militaristic focus with primarily tactical/kinetic responses.
	W3. There have been publicized incidents of police corruption.
S3. The police have demonstrated ability and susceptibility to evolve to a more community-focused organization.	W4. There have been publicized incidents of police brutality.
S4. The organization is large, with a lot of personnel resources.	W5. Organization is very autocratic and top-down; there is no decision-making authority at the line level.
	W6. Institutional resistance to change.

---

[3] Waddington, D. (2017) A SWOT Analysis of Community Policing as a Reform Schema For the Egyptian National Police To Counter Violent Extremism. University at Albany, Albany, New York

HELPFUL (EXTERNAL) to establishing encouraging narratives	HURTFUL (EXTERNAL) to establishing encouraging narratives
OPPORTUNITIES	THREATS
O1. When a police service focuses on improving relations with the public, it undermines the negative narrative that police are "the enemy".	T1. There is a history of distrust in the police that is not easily erased.
O2. International support and training is available to help the police organization transition to be more community focused.	T2. Successful/measurable police reform has proven to be difficult to achieve throughout the world.
O3. Community policing continues to be the preferred model for international police reform. Community policing has been proven to improve the image of the police.	T3. Community engagement takes a long time to implement.
	T4. It takes a lot of resources to effectively engage the community.
O4. There is a social media network in place that the police can take advantage of to challenge the negative narratives.	T5. Community policing and similar community-engagement programs requires autonomy and self-initiation for police in the field.
	T6. There is a well-established media campaign against the police.

In table 7.1, an obstacle in efforts to change a negative narrative appears under weaknesses: W4, "There have been publicized incidents of police and brutality." As long as communities view their police as brutal, it will be impossible to enhance public confidence and counter the negative narratives related to the police. If this is one of the issues an organization is prioritizing as part of an organizational change, the organization must also understand the nature of brutality in police organizations. For example, the only effective mechanism for addressing police brutality is top-down reform of the police organization. This includes introducing principles such as community policing; training officers in de-escalation skills and the use of nonlethal tactics; increasing the diversity of personnel within the organization; improving data collection and public transparency; and enhancing the screening of police recruits.

Many police organizations default to blaming "rogue cops," not organizational culture, for the perception of a brutal police service. Although claims of police abuse may cluster around a relatively small group of police officers, those officers tend to repeat their abusive behavior with impunity. Repeated brutality that is not addressed by higher-ups is a systemic problem, not a problem of rogue individuals. Whether or not it is explicit, the message is being conveyed by the organization that some level of abusive behavior is acceptable.

No police leader would instruct his or her officers to brutalize suspects. But certain features of police culture reward aggressive behavior or send a subliminal message that a certain amount of brutality is permitted or even necessary. Sometimes this mindset starts at the police academy, where cadets are taught that "complacency kills." But even when academy training avoids sending this message (by, for example, including instruction in de-escalation techniques), recruits soon buy into the model of aggressive, authoritative policing exhibited by some veterans on the force.

Moreover, the way departments emphasize quantitative performance has an effect on overall culture: metrics that place more value on crimes solved, arrests made, and tickets written than on harder-to-measure accomplishments such as dangerous situations diffused or avoided foster a certain ethos. By rewarding aggressive actions—which may even be dubbed heroic—such a system supports a style of policing that can escalate police-citizen confrontations. It also undermines the deterrent effects of citizen complaints or lawsuits, which are deemed "necessary evils" for effective crime fighting.

Police brutality resists reform because police assume that a certain level of violence is necessary in the situations they face, and organizational practice gives them the benefit of the doubt when applying force. The way officers interpret and employ violence is structured around institutional culture, impeding officers' ability to appreciate and correct errors in their use of force.

Reining in brutal behavior requires a change in police culture. Scholars agree that the organizational culture of policing (the set of informal norms that are unique to the policing profession) is the most important determinant of police behavior.[43] Changing the culture of an organization is hard; changing the culture of police services is particularly so; addressing the problem of police brutality, which may be seen as a component of police protecting themselves or administering justice, is especially difficult.

Other systemic recommendations urged by policing experts are more straightforward and actionable, and many departments have gradually made progress in implementing those suggestions. Among the recommendations that have helped make the culture of police organizations more community focused are the following:[5]

- Provide enhanced training for police officers on effective communication and community engagement. There is a consensus that more intelligent and better educated officers will exercise better judgment and be more effective.

- Conduct police visits to schools, such as those that are part of the U.S. "Officer Friendly" program, to improve the police's image and relations with young people; attend meetings of Parent Teacher Associations and similar organizations to meet and communicate with parents.

- Provide information—including about arrests and convictions—to ensure that the residents of a community know what is being

---

[4] J. Q. Wilson, *Varieties of Police Behavior: The Management of Law and Order in Eight Communities, With a New Preface by the Author* (Cambridge, MA: Harvard University Press, 1978).

[5] Drawn from Edwin Meese III and John Malcolm, *Policing in America: Lessons from the Past, Opportunities for the Future* (Washington, DC: Heritage Foundation, September 18, 2017), https://www.heritage.org/crime-and-justice/report/policing-america-lessons-the-past-opportunities-the-future.

done to address crime in their area. Information bulletins should describe not only enforcement actions but also the positive nonenforcement activities that police undertake.

- Focus data collection and performance metrics in areas that police services want to emphasize and in areas in need of improvement.

The Police Executive Research Forum (PERF), a nonprofit policy organization based in Washington, DC, analyzed a number of cases in which officers used excessive force as a first-resort means of addressing situations. PERF found that police services do not receive adequate training in communication, Daesh intervention, and nonviolent de-escalation of crises. Police need better training to be prepared to handle confrontations with the community in a way that improves, not worsens, community relations. Police officers also need training on dealing with community members in nonthreatening ways using better communication skills. If police are not properly trained, they will default to something they do know: the use of force. Although not a perfect solution, more comprehensive training for police officers provides a good start in addressing the problem of brutality. Police need to learn more than the logistics of policing. They also need to learn the broader significance of their role in society.[64]

However, such training requires an investment of resources that a police service may not have available. Consider what types of opportunities might help address this weakness. In particular, consider O2 in the opportunities quadrant: "International support and training is available to help the police organization transition to be more community focused." The agency may be able to take advantage of this opportunity.

The next step in tackling police brutality would be to use the SMART process to set appropriate goals for a training program to change the organizational culture and perception of brutality. Although a number of goals may be related to this issue (e.g., policy change, training), this chapter focuses on training. Recall that SMART stands for making goals that are specific, measurable, attainable, relevant, and timely.

---

[6] P. Swarts, "Police Need Better Training and Community Relations, Presidential Task Force Is Told," *Washington Times*, January 13, 2015.

Specific. The best way to ensure a goal is specific is by answering the five "W" questions:

- *What do we want to accomplish?* We want to change the police culture to one that does not tolerate brutality by retraining police personnel on appropriate use of force.
- *Why is this goal important?* Police personnel must have the understanding and techniques to use force only when necessary and at the appropriate level. Training will help to reduce potential incidents of brutality.
- *Who is involved?* All personnel—including management, supervisors, and line personnel—must receive training so that all understand; otherwise, the organizational culture will not change.
- *Where is it undertaken?* Training will occur at the training center.
- *Which resources or limits are involved?* It will require the participation of all personnel, which will mean changing some work shifts and making other adjustments. Funding will be required to support and implement the training.

Measurable. To illustrate that the goal is measurable, these questions must be answered:

- *How much do we want?* To retrain officers in the appropriate use of force, management would need two days to learn policy and rationale. For line personnel to learn policy, rationale, and techniques, and to practice techniques sufficiently to apply them appropriately, at least a full week is needed. (How much training is needed may vary, depending on the organization, but these time frames are fairly standard.)
- *How many do we want?* All personnel need to be trained to ensure cultural change.
- *How will we know when our goal is accomplished?* When all personnel are trained, this specific goal will be accomplished.

Achievable. To illustrate that the goal is measurable, the organization must answer these questions:

- *How can we accomplish this goal?* Training can be scheduled for all personnel. Potential assistance and funding might be available from international donors (as identified under opportunities on the SWOT matrix).
- *How realistic is the goal, based on other constraints?* If the agency is not able to finance and support the training itself, outside funding and other forms of support may be available. Personnel can be rotated in and out of training to ensure all receive it.

Relevant. To determine that a goal is relevant, these questions must be answered:

- *Does this seem worthwhile?* Yes, it will help establish a foundation for overcoming tendencies toward and accusations of brutality.
- *Is this the right time?* Yes; this should be one of the first steps in addressing the issue of brutality and the negative narrative associated with it.
- *Does this match our other efforts/needs?* Yes, training that is likely to overcome tendencies toward or accusations of brutality will support other efforts/needs.
- *Is it applicable in the current environment?* Yes, it addresses specific issues and needs as they relate to improving the police image.

Timely. To determine if the goal is time bound, the organization should ask these questions:

- *When?* Developing and implementing the training should occur as soon as possible.
- *What can we do six months from now?* Within six months, we should be able to begin training.
- *What can we do six weeks from now?* Within six weeks, we should be able to identify appropriate courses, training, potential international support, and associated funding.
- *What can we do now?* We can begin discussing with all levels of the organization the intent of implementing the training, as well as the rationale behind it.

Going through the SMART process for each goal identified through the SWOT analysis will ensure that those goals are in line with overall objectives and will maximize the likelihood that the goals are accomplished.

Conduct Training

The next step in the change process is training. Training builds skills and capabilities. Alongside communication, training is probably the most critical element of successful organizational change.

"Training" here does not refer specifically to the use-of-force training discussed above. "Training" is used here to refer to an essential component of the overall change process. There are several reasons why organizational training is essential in the organizational change process.

Increases the Rate of Change Success

Change management failures are often attributed to negative employee attitudes and unproductive management behavior. Because managers set behavioral standards in the workplace, managers must be on board with change and set the best example and tone for how change should be received by their teams. Police organizations should provide managers with training in change management and on how to advocate for change while providing appropriate support to the rank and file. During times of change, organizations should deliver refresher leadership training to ensure that managers are leading their people positively and productively.

Helps Maintain Visibility and Encourage a Sense of Belonging

In many organizations, employees have little understanding of how the organization actually operates. Key to engagement on the job is a sense of belonging, which comes from understanding the organizational environment. The organization should offer training that clearly shares with all employees the organization's mission, vision, values, and strategies; regular refresher courses can provide opportunities to commit these ideas to memory and embed them in daily operations.

It is important to engage and involve employees in the change management process. Managers should be trained in how to deliver a change message incrementally to their people; they should gather feedback from individuals and use this input to influence the change process by providing bottom-up insight.

Handling organizational change effectively will significantly reduce associated fear and negativity and stop associated rumors. Managers who receive training will be ready to support their personnel as they adjust to change and learn new ways of doing things while feeling secure in the process.

Draft and Implement a Change Plan

Once the organization has established goals and provided training, it can implement a plan to achieve those goals. One of the biggest problems in strategic planning is not following steps to implement a plan. Time and energy spent identifying where the organization is and determining where it wants to be are wasted without a plan that includes concrete steps. Strong leadership at this critical stage is key to successfully implementing a strategic plan.

An action plan sets forth the goals that have been established, specifies the steps needed to reach them, and identifies the entity responsible for accomplishing each one and within what time frame. This process ensures that the hard work of developing the strategic plan will become more than an exercise in wishful thinking. The difference between a wish and a goal is the initiation of an action plan that specifically outlines responsibilities for success. The following recommendations highlight ways of implementing change successfully.

- *Somebody has to be responsible*: A specific person must be responsible for seeing the plan through. This does not mean one person has to do all the work; it means that a single individual is held accountable for pushing the plan forward. The power, judgment, and authority to make the plan work need to abide in this one person.
- *Develop metrics throughout the plan:* Without metrics, the chances of successful completion drop off substantially. Midcourse

evaluations using those metrics can become the catalyst for revisiting the plan. Without a metrics, forward progress becomes objective.

- *If issues develop, understand the root causes and make adjustments:* It is not enough to know a plan is not working. Unanticipated conditions are part of any police environment. Rather than sticking with a plan that is not working, search for the root causes of the issues. Making wise adjustments to the plan is crucial to long-term success.

- *Insist on individual compliance with the plan:* Change is difficult and threatens senior officials more than junior officers. It is not uncommon for a senior official to oppose some aspect of a plan. Except in the most blatant of cases, this opposition manifests itself indirectly, with activities delayed or undertaken in a half-hearted fashion, undermining the overall plan and its objectives. Such obstructionism must be addressed at the individual level.

- *Instruct, educate, and coach throughout the plan:* Any plan—no matter how basic—must contain a mechanism for training those involved in the plan's execution. Training may not always be formal, but ongoing training and coaching will help ensure the plan is successfully implemented.

- *Adjust the plan as necessary to changing situations:* No plan is perfect. Even the best plan must be tweaked along the way. "Implementation, adaptation, implementation" is a useful mantra to recite throughout the change process

Overview of the Change Process

The change process starts when a stimulus for change (the need to increase public confidence in the police) leads to the identification of a target for change. The target is the actual system or procedure that is to change and is thus the subject of the change implementation that will be achieved through one or more stages. This target is identified through a SWOT analysis. This chapter has used the example of police brutality to demonstrate the process of change implementation.

As implementation progresses, observations and evaluations of the results provide feedback to the situation that originally gave rise to the stimulus for change, thereby enabling the organization to determine if it is actually making a difference.

If the system outputs satisfy the need for change, then the stimulus for change will reduce or disappear. If not, then the stimulus to change will modify, perhaps identifying a different target for change implementation; this process of modification will continue until the need is met and there are no further stimuli to change.[7]

Summary

The purpose of strategic planning is to help an organization understand where it is, where it wants to go, and how it can best get there. Although different organizations use varying terms for strategic planning, they should all focus on developing a thoughtful plan to achieve growth and success. Benjamin Franklin supposedly said, "If you fail to plan, you are planning to fail." The wisdom of this aphorism is particularly relevant for organizations that face numerous challenges and competing priorities. The police profession cannot afford to practice "pinball leadership," getting bounced around by every unexpected event. Instead, leaders must plan proactively, mapping a path that will lead to the future they envision for the organization

The objectives of any police organization contemplating change should be to manage change in a manner that offers the greatest possibility of success without reducing the quality and quantity of service to the public; indeed, the change should *increase* the quality and the quantity of service. A primary objective of CVE-oriented policing is to establish and strengthen the bonds between the police and the communities they are supposed to serve.

---

[7] J. M. Hart, "The Management of Change in Police Organizations," in *Policing in Central and Eastern Europe: Comparing Firsthand Knowledge with Experience from the West,* ed. Milan Pagon (Ljubljana, Slovenia: College of Police and Security Studies, 1996)

CHAPTER 8
CONCLUSION

NADIA GERSPACHER

This field manual offers a roadmap for police services that wish to professionalize their narrative and thus enhance their CVE capacity. The preceding chapters provide guidance on developing positive messages to encourage communities to collaborate with police and to contribute to collective resilience to the pull of violent extremist messages and activities. The book highlights key components of a strategy for creating positive messages to foster a collaborative environment between police and the communities they aim to serve. By engaging in a continuous dialogue with each other, the police and their communities can become guardians of collective security.

This field manual underlines the importance of understanding violent extremist narratives and the key reasons for their resonance with communities so that police can leverage the same values in their positive messages. Violent extremist narratives differ from community to community. Police organizations must understand the messages of violent extremist groups in their communities and why these narratives are effective at garnering support for the use of violence. Countering violent extremists' messages also requires an understanding of the motivation of these groups, the stories they aim to tell, and how these groups interpret and depict events in the community, including police operations and the use of force. Police need to understand the nature of the appeal of extremist messages so they can better understand their communities and become more relevant interlocutors. Developing and diffusing positive messages are part of a larger strategy to develop meaningful partnerships that privilege addressing the underlying problems in a community. A focus on partnerships and problem solving are the cornerstones of a community-oriented policing ethos.

Police must invest time and resources (mostly human) in understanding the master narratives of violent extremists. The vocabulary used in these narratives provides communities with the means to describe their society, their police, and their government. Violent extremist messages work for various reasons. They may satisfy a deep-seated need for security not provided by the government; they may create a sense of belonging; they may resonate with community members' specific views and beliefs; and they may confirm biases and fears about the "other." Understanding extremist narratives helps police understand their own community and what issues to address through partnerships. Police can then use their narratives to siphon support from violent extremist groups.

Police narratives depend first and foremost on the ability of the organization to conduct itself in a professional manner. To that end, police services need to conduct regular assessments of their strengths and weaknesses. Behavior, conduct, and activities that delegitimize the police can promote and even fuel violent extremist narratives. Positive messages can be crafted only on the observable capacity of police to serve communities professionally. It is important to keep up with the changing perceptions and attitudes of communities and use candid assessments to guide the organizational change required to enhance the confidence of the community in the police. Police services should constantly ask themselves questions such as, how do communities perceive the police? How likely are they to call the police in time of need? Honest answers to these kinds of questions provide information about the confidence communities have in their police and how resilient they can be together in the fight to counter violent extremist narratives. Positive messages must be backed up on the street—proven by police conduct. Police should avoid disseminating positive messages that are disproven by stories of community members having negative interactions with the police.

Adopting a community-oriented policing ethos requires the development of partnerships that result in a network of services to provide solutions to problems that, if left unchecked, could become grievances. Marginalization is a key contributor to recruitment into and support for violent extremist movements. Young people at risk of being radicalized, for example, are a key subgroup who should be included in a network of partnerships and enlisted to help address problems in the community. They can be considered in both the prevention of and the response to violent extremist activities and can be important partners who can offer specific insights.

It is crucial for police to take an inclusive approach toward the many different groups that can be of assistance and provide those groups with access to the police (not for purposes of intelligence gathering, but for purposes of prevention). Police should expand partnerships across all subgroups in society and across government agencies that can act as allies in finding solutions to problems in the community. Creating and implementing solutions and preventing grievances also requires effective messaging strategies. Without them, partnerships are less broadly impactful.

Messages that are promoted online have the potential to reach audiences that might be hard to reach in person. Social media can be used to share stories of protection, to humanize public perceptions of police, and to promote a vocabulary and a mindset about the police to the community. Social media can also communicate the nature and scope of police activities in a community-focused and service-driven light. When community members use the language of protection embedded in the police narrative, they give more legitimacy to the police, which in turn allows the police to introduce doubt about the reliability of the violent extremist narrative. With these tools and a willingness to engage communities and invite them to collaborate on CVE, police can make it a priority to develop an engagement strategy.

The key ingredients in that strategy are the capacity to communicate using messages and a vocabulary that include key objectives in CVE; to relay to the community the core values of the police service; and to explain to community members the role of the police and what can be expected from individual officers. This strategy privileges transparency in the police service's efforts to protect communities form the violence of violent extremist organizations. If the police service's positive messages are to be accepted by the community, the entire service has to earn the community's confidence in its ability to conduct operations that provide security without excessive use of force. This requires that the police service adopt a mindset that is visible throughout the organization, its policies and its practices, its vocabulary, and the conduct of every officer. In order to be able to develop messages of protection and of two-way collaboration with community members, the police organization needs to show that it has earned the trust and confidence of the community and has been granted the community's consent to be policed.

The communication and engagement activities of police need to be built on practices that may require an organizational shift of competencies, resources, goals, and metrics. These shifts will turn the police service into an outward-looking organization that solicits the cooperation of other government institutions and of all groups within the communities. CVE policing requires officers to recognize that they are relatively powerless without wide engagement. The overall goal of community-oriented policing in CVE efforts is to ally with all relevant individuals and groups to create a resilient community that perceives its police as the best defense against violent extremism. Narratives can be used to establish and maintain these partnerships.